Oedipus the King

and

Antigone

Crofts Classics

GENERAL EDITOR
Samuel H. Beer, *Harvard University*

SOPHOCLES

Oedipus the King
and
Antigone

Translated and Edited by
Peter D. Arnott
Tufts University

Harlan Davidson, Inc.
Wheeling, Illinois 60090-6000

Library of Congress Cataloging-in-Publication Data

Sophocles.
    Oedipus, the King; and Antigone.
    (Crofts classics)
    Bibliography: p. 107
1. Sophocles—Translations, English. 2. Oedipus (Greek mythology) Drama.
3. Antigone (Legendary character)—Drama. I. Arnott, Peter D. II. Sophocles.
Antigone. English. 1987. III. Title. IV. Title: Oedipus, the King. V. Title:
Antigone.
PA4414.A2A7   1987   882'.01   87-13603
ISBN 0-88295-094-0 (pbk.)

Manufactured in the United States of America
99 98 97 35 36 37 CM

introduction

Sophocles, the second great figure in the history of Greek, and thus of all, drama, was born in Colonus, a suburb of Athens. Like most Greek writers he played a full part in public life. There was as yet no conception of a professional theater in the modern commercial sense. Performances were limited in Athens to three main festivals each year, and associated with an act of public worship. Sophocles was an amateur in the noblest sense of the word, writing not for financial reward but for the love of his art and the honor of public recognition. Moreover, the poet was still regarded as a teacher, whose function was not merely to entertain but to provide his audiences with matter for reflection. Thus tragedy, while taking its subjects from a body of familiar stories, employs these stories as a framework within which to treat pertinent moral problems. Sophocles' work is a commentary upon the main currents of thought in his own time.

His life covered a period of profound change in Athens and the Greek world generally. The traditional religion, never completely satisfactory, was becoming more and more the target of criticism. Interest was shifting from the nature of the gods to the nature of man himself, his triumphs and tragedies, powers and limitations. In the works of Sophocles, and particularly in the two plays in this volume, this new humanism finds perhaps its purest and most profound expression, without the bitter cynicism we observe in the plays of Euripides, his near contemporary.

SOPHOCLES AND THE DEVELOPMENT OF TRAGEDY

Tragedy had evolved from its primitive beginnings in dance-drama and sacred songs to become a highly formal art in which the story was told through an alternation of acted scenes and choruses. The number of actors was always limited—before Sophocles to two—though one actor might take several parts in the play; and emphasis had lain chiefly on the chorus. To Sophocles is ascribed the introduction of the third actor. This opened the way for more complex scenes and greater possibilities of characterization, and the importance of the chorus was thereby diminished. Sophocles may therefore be said to have invented character in an art form which had previously been concerned mainly with theme. It is significant that another tradition credits him with being the first to write parts with particular actors in mind. This shift of emphasis from mass spectacle to individual characterization reflects the growing awareness of human personality and motivation.

The plays were written to be performed in an open-air theater devoid of scenic artifice. The focal point was the orchestra, a circular space in which the chorus sang and danced. Round most of this circle ran the steeply raked auditorium. On the far side stood the scene building (skēnē) with a painted architectural façade and a low platform on which the actors performed, connected by steps with the orchestra. As in Shakespeare's theater the scene was set by the dramatist's words. He had only to suggest where the action was taking place, and the imagination of the audience did the rest. Against this multi-purpose background the actors, wearing formalized masks and ornate robes, declaimed their parts, with the action punctuated by choral songs. The music of these Greek plays has been lost to us, but it is important to realize that the manner of stage presentation was as formal as the manner of composition. Greek tragedy offered a unique combination of music, dancing, and the spoken word. To find an equivalent we must look not to the modern theater in Europe and America but to the traditional drama forms of the Orient.

THE LEGEND

The story of Oedipus appears in Greek literature as early as Homer, and soon passed into the poetic heritage, undergoing several modifications until at last it reached the hands of the dramatists. The version used by Sophocles is as follows.

It was prophesied to Laius and Jocasta, King and Queen of Thebes, that the son to be born to them would murder his father and marry his own mother. To avert this disaster they exposed the child with his feet pinned together (hence the name Oedipus, "swollen-foot") to die on the mountain side. He was found by a kindly shepherd and taken to Corinth, where he was adopted by the childless Polybus and Merope and brought up as a prince of the royal house. Learning of the prophecy uttered at his birth, he fled his supposed parents in terror. His wanderings brought him back to Thebes. On the way he killed in a roadside brawl an old man who, unknown to him, was King Laius. Thebes was ravaged by the Sphinx, a monster half-beast half-woman, who killed anyone who could not answer her riddle. Oedipus solved it, defeated the Sphinx, and was rewarded with the hand of the widowed Jocasta and the Theban throne. There he ruled in peace and prosperity until the coming of a plague which could only be removed by the discovery of Laius' murderer. Here begins the action of Oedipus the King, and the chain of circumstances which finally reveals to Oedipus the secret of his birth. Oedipus blinded himself and left Thebes to wander in exile, dying in Colonus (the subject of Oedipus at Colonus, not included in this volume). Thebes was ravaged by civil war, in which Oedipus' two sons, Eteocles and Polyneices, fought and killed each other. Creon, Jocasta's brother, ascended to the throne. Here Antigone begins, telling of Creon's refusal to bury Polyneices and its tragic consequences.

THE PLAYS

Although dealing with successive episodes in the same story the Oedipus plays were not conceived as a unity but written at different points in Sophocles' career. Although, for the sake of clarity, they are printed in the order of the story here, Antigone was in fact written first, in about 441 B.C., then Oedipus the King in about 429 B.C., and finally Oedipus at Colonus, the work of Sophocles' last years, produced posthumously in 401 B.C. They must therefore be regarded as independent compositions, and the reader must not expect to find consistency of characterization between one play and another, or even that the details of the story tally. The Creon of Oedipus the King, for example, differs markedly from the Creon of Antigone. But these discrepancies are irrelevant. It is simply a question of focus. In each play Sophocles has something new to say, and adapts the details of the story to his immediate purpose.

Antigone has been interpreted variously as a conflict between divine and human law, between family and state, between generosity and intolerance. Superficially the issue is simple. Creon finds it politically expedient to deny burial to the traitor Polyneices; Antigone, claiming that the right of burial transcends all other considerations, performs the last rites over her brother's body and is condemned to death. For the Greeks, to refuse a man burial was the worst of crimes, sentencing him to wander forever a homeless shade, denied entrance to the underworld. Although these associations have now lost something of their force, modern audiences would be no less ready to support Antigone against Creon. Are we then to regard the play as the story of a persecuted heroine? Several considerations argue against this romantic conception. Creon suffers no less than Antigone, and it is with his personal tragedy that the latter part of the play is concerned. Let us say rather that Sophocles has shown us here two strong-willed people in conflict. Neither is selfish; both have a clear conception of where their duty lies, and are resolved to obey its dictates. But Creon's views are too narrow. In achieving his immediate purpose he has blinded himself to more fundamental obligations. Nor is Antigone herself above criticism. If we close our eyes for a moment to the pathos of her situation, we see that Sophocles has not made her particularly sympathetic—note her treatment of Ismene in the opening dialogue, and her callous disregard of Haemon, the boy who will lay down his life for her. Creon's failing is his stubbornness, his refusal to go back on a misguided decision once he has made it; Antigone's, that she is too impatient when faced with human frailty, that she refuses even to attempt appeals and persuasion.

Possibly the greatest problem in interpretation of Antigone has been that of the "double burial." Polyneices' corpse is covered twice, the first time by a mysterious sprinkling of dust. Antigone is caught red-handed making the second attempt. Perhaps the most attractive explanation is that the first "burial" is a natural phenomenon sent by the gods as a warning to Creon, a warning he chooses to ignore.

Oedipus the King, concentrating on a single character, is in many respects a more powerful tragedy than Antigone. Sophocles here develops, in a tightly-knit plot, themes we have already seen in the earlier work. The mechanics of the plot are powerful enough in themselves. Sophocles has contrived, while dealing with the immediate action, to keep the background constantly in our minds. Past and present are skillfully intertwined, until all the threads are tied together in Oedipus' moment of self-revelation.

Stubbornness is inherent in Oedipus' character as it was in Creon's. In Oedipus, however, this failing is balanced by the corresponding virtue of persistence. He too can make a misguided decision—his accusation of Teiresias and Creon—and cling to it; but his virtue is his ability to go on questioning to the bitter end, even after the first premonitions of disaster. Oedipus is a man who must know the truth at all costs. Teiresias warns him, early in the play, that the truth may be terrible, but he is still impelled to seek it out. His weakness, his "fatal flaw," is his belief that the human intellect is sufficient to itself. His pride in his past achievements, his acknowledged intellectual superiority, mislead him into thinking that cleverness is the same thing as wisdom. The events which his investigation sets in train prove to him that this is not so. Nevertheless he meets his self-inflicted disaster grandly. His self-blinding is not an act of weakness but of strength. Jocasta, superficially the stronger character, is the first to crack. She cannot face the truth, but commits suicide. Oedipus is strong enough to face the truth and go on living. His is the true strength, the strength to learn from suffering, and he ends the play a nobler character than he began it. His self-conceit has been purged and he has won through to a deeper understanding.

Sophocles plays continually on the opposition of light and darkness, sight and blindness. In the Teiresias scene, Oedipus is revealed as mentally blind to his real position and the dangers which surround him. It is the blind prophet who has true knowledge. At the end of the play, when Oedipus has found the truth, he destroys the fallible sense organs which had led him into error. He is now blind, but sees truly.

The tragedy of Oedipus is thus a hymn to man, who for all his limitations and propensities to error still possesses a grandeur which is all his own and owes nothing to the gods. Both Antigone and Oedipus, in spite of all, end nobly. Sophocles was not concerned with delineating every aspect of the human character. There is nothing petty or mean about his protagonists. They are still superhuman figures, moving in a world of great issues, purged of the triviality of our own. Nevertheless Sophocles has created characters with whom we can suffer and sympathize, in whom we can see the virtues and vices of humanity written large.

principal dates in the life
of Sophocles

B.C. 495   Birth of Sophocles

480   Chosen to lead the chorus celebrating the Greek victory over Persia at Salamis

468   Production of the lost *Triptolemus*; defeats Aeschylus in the dramatic festival

?   Production of *Ajax*

443/1   Production of *Antigone*

440   Appointed general, serves on expedition against the island of Samos

?   Production of *The Women of Trachis*

431   *Outbreak of war between Athens and Sparta*

?429   Production of *Oedipus the King*

?   Production of *Electra*

409   Production of *Philoctetes*

406   Death of Sophocles

401   Posthumous production of *Oedipus at Colonus*

OEDIPUS THE KING

dramatis personae

Priest
Oedipus, King of Thebes
Creon, brother of Jocasta
Chorus of Theban elders
Teiresias, a blind prophet
Jocasta, wife of Oedipus
First Messenger
Herdsman
Second Messenger

Antigone and Ismene, daughters of Oedipus and
Jocasta (nonspeaking parts)

Citizens of Thebes, Attendants

Scene: Before the palace of Oedipus in Thebes.

OEDIPUS THE KING

❧

[*A crowd of Theban citizens—priests, young
men and children—kneel in supplication before the palace, wearing wreaths and carrying
branches. Enter* OEDIPUS *from the palace to
address them.*]

OEDIPUS. My children, in whom old Cadmus is re-
   born,
Why have you come with wreathed boughs in your
   hands
To sit before me as petitioners?
The town is full of smoke from altar-fires
And voices crying, and appeals to heaven.
I thought it, children, less than just to hear
Your cause at second-hand, but come in person—
I, Oedipus, a name that all men know.
Speak up, old man; for you are qualified
To be their spokesman. What is in your minds?   10,
Are you afraid? In need? Be sure I am ready
To do all I can. I should truly be hard-hearted
To have no pity on such prayers as these.
   PRIEST. Why, Oedipus, my country's lord and master,

1 **Cadmus** legendary founder of Thebes. He killed the dragon
guarding the site and sowed its teeth in the ground. From them
sprang up armed men who fought each other. All were killed
except five, who became the ancestors of the Thebans.   2
wreathed boughs branches entwined with wool, the customary
symbol of supplication

5

You see us, of all ages, sitting here
Before your altars—some too young to fly
Far from the nest, and others bent with age,
Priests—I of Zeus—and these, who represent
Our youth. The rest sit with their boughs
20 In the city squares, at both of Pallas' shrines,
And where Ismenus' ashes tell the future.
The storm, as you can see, has hit our land
Too hard; she can no longer raise her head
Above the waves of this new sea of blood.
A blight is on the blossoms of the field,
A blight is on the pastured herds, on wives
In childbed; and the curse of heaven, plague,
Has struck, and runs like wildfire through the city,
Emptying Cadmus' house, while black Death reaps
30 The harvest of our tears and lamentations.
Not that we see you as a god, these boys
And I, who sit here at your feet for favors,
But as one pre-eminent in life's affairs
And in man's dealings with the powers above.
For it was you who came to Cadmus' town
And freed us from the monster who enslaved us
With her song, relying on your wits, and knowing
No more than we. Some god was at your side,
As men believe, when you delivered us.
40 So now, great Oedipus, giant among men,
We beg you, all of us who come in prayer,
Find us some remedy—a whisper heard
From heaven, or any human way you know.
In men proved by experience we see
A living promise, both in word and deed.

18 **Zeus** king of the gods   20 **Pallas** Athena, goddess of wisdom   21 **Ismenus** river near Thebes. Here the reference is to the prophetic shrine of Apollo by the river, where divination by burnt offerings was practised   36 **the monster . . . her song** the Sphinx and the riddle.

Greatest of men, give our city back its pride!
Look to your name! This country now remembers
Your former zeal, and hails you as her savior.
Never leave us with a memory of your reign
As one that raised and let us fall again,   50
But lift our city up, and keep it safe.
You came to make us happy years ago,
Good omens; show you are the same man still.
If you continue in your present power
Better a land with citizens than empty.
For city walls without their men are nothing,
Or empty ships, when once the crew has gone.
   OED. Poor children, I already know too well
The desires that bring you here. Yes, I have seen
Your sufferings; but suffer as you may,   60
There is not one of you who knows my pain.
Your griefs are private, every man here mourns
For himself, and for no other; but my heart grieves
At once for the state, and for myself, and you.
So do not think you rouse me from my sleep.
Let me tell you, I have wept, yes, many tears,
And sent my mind exploring every path.
My anxious thought found but one hope of cure
On which I acted—sent Creon, Menoeceus' son,
My own wife's brother, to Apollo's shrine   70
At Delphi, with commission to enquire
What I could say or do to save this town.
Now I am counting the days, and growing anxious
To know what he is doing. It is strange
He should delay so long beyond his time.
But when he comes, I shall be no true man
If I fail to take the course the god has shown us

70 **Apollo's shrine at Delphi** most famo[us]
Greek oracular shrines, believed to stan[d]
center of the earth

PRIEST. Well said, and timely! My friends are signal-
  ing
This very moment that Creon is in sight.
80   OED. O Lord Apollo, let him bring us news
Glad as his face, to give our town good fortune.
    PRIEST. I think he brings us comfort; otherwise
He would not wear so thick a crown of laurel.

[*Enter* CREON]

OED. We shall soon know, he is close enough to hear
  us.
Prince, brother of my house, Menoeceus' son,
What is the news you bring us from the god?
    CREON. Good news! Our sorrows, heavy as they are,
With proper care may yet end happily.
    OED. What is the oracle? So far you have said noth-
  ing
90 To raise my spirits or to dampen them.
    CREON. If you wish to have it here and now, in pub-
  lic,
I am ready to speak; if not, to go inside.
    OED. Speak before all. The sorrows of my people
I count of greater weight than life itself.
    CREON. Then, by your leave, I speak as I was told.
Phoebus commands us, in plain terms, to rid
Our land of some pollution, nourished here,
He says, and not to keep a thing past cure.
    OED. How shall we purge ourselves? What stain is
  this?
100   CREON. By banishing a man, or taking life
For life, since murder brought this storm on us.
    OED. Who is the man whose fate the god reveals?
    CREON. Our country once had Laius for its king,

83 **crown of laurel** leaves from Apollo's sacred tree   96 **Phoebus**
Apollo

My lord, before you came to guide this city.

OED. I have been told as much; I never saw him.

CREON. Laius was murdered. Phoebus tells us plainly
To find his murderers and punish them.

OED. Where on earth are they? An ancient crime,
A scent grown cold; where shall we find it now?

CREON. Here, in this land, he said; seek it, and we   110
Shall find; seek not, and it shall be hidden.

OED. And where did Laius meet his bloody end?
In the country? The palace? Traveling abroad?

CREON. He left us on a visit, as he said,
To Delphi, and he never came back home.

OED. Could no-one tell you? Had he no companion,
No witness, who could give you facts to work on?

CREON. All were killed but one, who ran away in
   fright,
And will swear to only one thing that he saw.

OED. What was that? One thing might give the clue
   to more   120
If we had some encouragement, some small beginning.

CREON. He said they met with bandits; it was not
By one man's hands that Laius died, but many.

OED. What bandit would have taken such a risk
Unless he were bribed—by someone here, in Thebes?

CREON. It was suspected; but then our troubles came
And there was no-one to avenge dead Laius.

OED. It must have been great trouble, that could
   make you
Leave the death of royalty unsolved!

CREON. The Sphinx, whose riddles made us turn our
   minds   130
To things at home, and abandon mysteries.

OED. Then I shall start afresh, and once again
Find secrets out. Apollo and you too
Have rightly taken up the dead man's cause.

You will see me working with you, as is just,
To avenge the land, and give the god his due.
It is not on some far-distant friend's behalf
But on my own, that I shall purge this stain.
The man whose hand killed Laius might some time
140 Feel a desire to do the same to me,
And so by avenging him I protect myself.
Waste no more time, my children, take away
Your branches and your wreaths, and leave my steps.
Have Cadmus' people summoned here and tell them
I will see to everything. We shall be happy now,
God helping us, or be forever damned.

[*Exeunt* OEDIPUS *and* CREON]

PRIEST. Let us arise, my sons. He promises
The favors that we first came here to ask.
May Phoebus who has sent this oracle
150 Come to save Thebes, and cure us of the plague!

[*Exeunt. Enter* CHORUS *of Theban elders*]

CHORUS. Sweet voice of Zeus, what word do you
     bring
From golden Pytho to glorious Thebes?
I am heart-shaken, torn on the rack of fear.
Apollo, Healer, to whom men cry,
I tremble before you; what will it please you
To send us? Some new visitation?
Or something out of the past, come due
In fullness of time? Tell me, Voice undying,
The child of golden Hope.

160 Daughter of Zeus, to you first I cry,
Immortal Athena; and then her sister

152 **Pytho** Delphi

Artemis, guardian of our land, enthroned
In honor in our assemblies; Apollo,
Heavenly archer; now shine on us all three,
Champions strong against death; if ever
In time gone by you stood between Thebes
And threatened disaster, turning the fire
Of pestilence from us, come now!

For my sorrows have grown past counting.
The plague is on all our people, and wit   170
Can devise no armor. No more the good earth
Brings forth its crops; women groan in their barren la-
        bors,
And you may see, like flying birds,
Souls speeding, one by one,
To join the sunset god; their flight
Is faster than the racing flame.

Thebes dies a new death each moment; her children
Lie in the dust, death's agents, and no-one
Spares them a tear; their wives and gray-haired moth-
        ers
Flock screaming to the altars, and pray for their own
        lives.   180
Above the counterpoint of tears
There rings out clear the healing chant.
Show us, golden child of Zeus,
The smiling face of comfort!

Grim Death is marching on us, not now with clashing
        shields
But blasts of fiery breath, and the cry goes up around
        him.

162 **Artemis** goddess of childbirth and of wild things

Turn him away from us, drive him from our land!
Come, fair wind, and blow him away
To the vasty halls of the western ocean
190 Or the Thracian seas, where sailors fear to go.
For if night has left any harm undone
Day treads on its heels to finish the work.
Zeus our Father, lord of the bright lightning,
Come with your thunder and destroy!

And we pray Apollo the archer to string his golden bow
And send invincible arrows to fight for us in the field,
And Artemis' blazing torches, that she carries
To light her way through the Lycian mountains.
On the god with gold-bound hair I call,
200 Bacchus, whose name we have made our own,
Who comes with a cry of maidens dancing.
Bright comforter, bring the joyous light
Of your torch, stand with us against our foe,
The rogue-god, whom his brothers shun!

[*Enter* OEDIPUS]

OED. You pray; now for answer. If you are prepared
To accept what I say, and be your own physician,
Cure may be yours, and respite from your pain.
I must speak as a stranger to your story, one
Unacquainted with the facts; I could not press
210 My enquiries far alone, without some clue.
But now I am a Theban among Thebans
And make this proclamation to the sons
Of Cadmus: if anyone among you knows

190 **Thracian seas** off the north-east coast of Greece, notoriously treacherous. Ares, god of war, was regarded as having his home in this wild region.   198 **Lycian mountains** in Asia Minor   200 **Bacchus** Dionysus, god of wine, traditionally born in Thebes from the union of Zeus and a mortal woman, Semele

Who murdered Laius, son of Labdacus,
I order him to make a full disclosure.
If he should fear to implicate himself
By confessing, why, nothing unpleasant will happen;
He will leave the land unharmed, and that is all.
If anybody knows another guilty—
An alien perhaps—then let him not keep silent.   220
He will earn a reward and my gratitude besides.
But if you refuse to talk; if anyone
Is frightened into shielding self or friend,
Pay good attention to the consequences.
As lord and master of this land of Thebes
I declare this man, whoever he may be
An outlaw; order you to break off speech
With him, to excommunicate him from your prayers
And sacrifices, to deny him holy water,
To drive him from your doors, remembering   230
That this is our pollution, which the god
This day revealed to me in oracles.
In this I show myself on heaven's side,
One with the murdered man. My solemn curse
Is on the killer, whether he is hiding
In lonely guilt or has accomplices.
May he reap the harm he sowed, and die unblest.
And what is more, I pray that if this man
Should live among my household with my knowledge,
The curse I swore just now should fall on me.   240
I lay the responsibility on you,
For my sake, and the gods', and for our country
Turned to a stricken, god-forsaken waste.
For even if heaven had not shown its hand
Fitness alone forbade such negligence
When one so noble, and your king, had died.
You should have held enquiries. Now since I
Have fallen heir to the power which once was his,

Sleep in his bed, and take his bride to wife,
250 And since, if he had not been disappointed
In his succession, we two would have had
A bond between us, children of one mother,
But as it was, his fortune struck him down,
For all these reasons, I shall fight for him
As I would for my own father, leave no stone
Unturned to find the man who shed his blood
In honor of the son of Labdacus,
Of Polydorus, Cadmus, and Agenor.
For those who disobey my words I pray
260 The gods to send no harvest to their fields,
Their wives no children, but to let them die
In present misery, or worse to come.
But as for you, the rest of Cadmus' children,
Who think as I do, may our ally, Right,
And all the gods be with you evermore.

CHORUS. You put me on my oath and I must speak.
I did not kill him, nor can I point to the man
Who did. It was for Phoebus, who sent the question,
To answer it, and find the murderer.

270　OED. What you say is fair enough, but no man living
Can force the gods to speak when they do not want to.

CHORUS. By your leave, a second best occurs to
me. . . .

OED. Second or third best, do not keep it from us!

CHORUS. I know Teiresias has powers of vision
Second only to Phoebus. A man who asked of him,
My lord, might find his questions answered.

OED. Another thing that I have not neglected.
On Creon's bidding I have sent men twice
To bring him; it is strange he is not yet come.

CHORUS. We have nothing else but vague and ancient
280　rumors.

OED. What are they? I must examine every story.

CHORUS. He is said to have been killed by men on the
    road.
OED. Yes, so I hear; but no-one knows who did it.
CHORUS. If he has any fear in him, a curse
Such as you swore will bring him out of hiding.
    OED. Words will not scare a man when actions do
    not.
    CHORUS. But here is one to convict him. They are
    bringing
The prophet here at last, the man of god,
The only one who has the truth born in him.

[*Enter* TEIRESIAS, *led by a boy*]

    OED. Teiresias, all things are known to you,   290
Open and secret, things of heaven and earth.
Blind though you are, you sense how terrible
A plague is on us; and in you, great prophet,
We find our only means of self-defence.
We sent—perhaps my messengers have told you—
To Phoebus; he replied, by one way only
Could Thebes secure deliverance from the plague,
By hunting down the murderers of Laius
And killing them or driving them abroad.
So grudge us nothing of your bird-cry lore   300
Or any means of prophecy you know.
Come, save the city; save yourself and me,
And heal the foulness spread by Laius' blood.
We are in your hands. Man knows no finer task
Than helping friends with all his might and means.
    TEIRESIAS. How terrible is wisdom when it turns
Against you! All of this I know, but let it
Slip from my mind, or I should not have come here.

300 **bird-cry lore** omens were commonly deduced from the
flight of birds

OED. What is it? Why have you come in so black a
mood?

310   TEIR. Send me home. It will be easiest for each of us
To bear his own burden to the end, believe me.

OED. A fine way to talk! You do your motherland
No kindness by witholding information.

TEIR. When I see you opening your mouth at the
wrong moment
I take care to avoid a like mistake.

OED. By heaven, if you know something, do not turn
away!
You see us all on our knees imploring you.

TEIR. Yes, for you all know nothing. I shall never
Reveal my sorrows—not to call them yours.

320   OED. What do you say? You know and will not talk?
Do you mean to turn traitor and betray the state?

TEIR. I wish to cause no pain—to either of us.
So why ask useless questions? My lips are sealed.

OED. Why, you old reprobate, you could provoke
A stone to anger! Will you never speak?
Can nothing touch you? Is there no end to this?

TEIR. You blame my temper, but you fail to recognize
Your own working in you; no, you criticize me!

OED. And who would not be angry when he hears
you
330 Talking like this, and holding Thebes in contempt?

TEIR. These things will happen, if I speak or not.

OED. Then if they must, it is your duty to tell me.

TEIR. This discussion is at an end. Now, if you like,
You may be as angry as your heart knows how.

OED. Then in my anger I will spare you none
Of my suspicions. This is what I think;
You helped contrive the plot—no, did it all

Except the actual killing. If you had
Your eyesight I should say you did that too.

TEIR. Indeed? Then listen to what I say. Obey
Your own pronouncement, and from this day on   340
Speak not to me or any man here present.
You are the curse, the defiler of this land.

OED. You dare fling this at me? Have you no fear?
Where can you hope for safety after this?

TEIR. I am safe enough. My strength is in my truth.

OED. Who put you up to this? No skill of yours!

TEIR. You did—by forcing me to speak against my
will.

OED. What was it? Say it again, I must be sure.

TEIR. Did you not understand? Or are you tempting
me?

OED. I have not quite grasped it. Tell it me again.   350

TEIR. You hunt a murderer; it is yourself.

OED. You will pay for uttering such slanders twice.

TEIR. Shall I say something else, to make you angrier
still?

OED. Say what you like, it is a waste of breath.

TEIR. You have been living in unimagined shame
With your nearest, blind to your own degradation.

OED. How long do you think such taunts will go unpunished?

TEIR. For ever, if there is any strength in truth.

OED. In truth, but not in you. You have no strength,
Failing in sight, in hearing, and in mind.

TEIR. And you are a fool to say such things to me,   360
Things that the world will soon hurl back at you!

OED. You live in the dark; you are incapable
Of hurting me or any man with eyes.

TEIR. Your destiny is not to fall by me.
That is Apollo's task, and he is capable.

OED. Who is behind this? You? Or is it Creon?

TEIR. Your ruin comes not from Creon, but yourself.
OED. Oh wealth! Oh monarchy! Talent which out-
    runs
370 Its rivals in the cutthroat game of life,
How envy dogs your steps, and with what strength,
When tempted by the power the city gave
Into my hands, a gift, and never asked for,
The man I trusted, Creon, my earliest friend,
Yearns to depose me, plots behind my back,
Makes accomplices of conjurers like this
Who sells his tricks to the highest bidder, who looks
Only for profits, and in his art is blind.
Let us hear where you have proved yourself a seer!
380 Why did you not, when the Singing Bitch was here,
Utter one word to set your people free?
For this was not a riddle to be solved
By the first-comer; it cried out for divination.
You were tried and found wanting; neither birds
Nor voices from heaven could help you. Then I came,
I, ignorant Oedipus, and put a stop to her
By using my wits, no lessons from the birds!
And it is I you try to depose, assuming
That you will have a place by Creon's throne.
390 You and your mastermind will repent your zeal
To purge this land. You are old, by the look of you;
If not, you would have learnt the price of boldness.
    CHORUS. It seems to me that this man's words were
      spoken
In anger, Oedipus, and so were yours.
This is not what we need; we ask to know
How we can best obey the oracle.
    TEIR. King though you are, the right of speech must
      be

380 **Singing Bitch** the Sphinx

The same for all. Here, I am my own master.
I live in Apollo's service, not in yours,
And have no need of Creon to endorse me.   400
Listen to me; you taunt me with my blindness,
But you have eyes, and do not see your sorrows,
Or where you live, or what is in your house.
Do you know whose son you are? You are abhorrent
To your kin on earth and under it, and do not know.
One day your mother's and your father's curse,
A two-tongued lash, will run you out of Thebes,
And you who see so well will then be blind.
What place will not give shelter to your cries?
What corner of Cithairon will not ring with them,   410
When you have understood the marriage song which
    brought you
From prosperous voyage to uneasy harbor?
And a throng of sorrows that you cannot guess
Will drag you down and level you with those
You have begotten, and your proper self.
So go your way; heap mockery and insult
On Creon and my message; you will be crushed
More miserably than any man on earth.

    OED. Am I to listen to such things from him
Without protest? Out of my sight this instant! Leave
    my house!   420
Go back where you came from, and be damned!

    TEIR. I would never have come here, if you had not
    called me.

    OED. If I had known you would rave like this, it
    would have been
A long time before I asked you to my house.

    TEIR. I am what I am. I pass for a fool to you,
But as sane enough for the parents who begot you.

410 **Cithairon** mountain near Thebes where Oedipus was exposed

OED. Who were they? Wait! What is my father's
name?

TEIR. This day will give you parents and destroy
you.

OED. All the time you talk in riddles, mysteries.

430   TEIR. And who can decipher riddles better than you?

OED. Yes, laugh at that! There you will find my
greatness!

TEIR. And it is just this luck that has destroyed you.

OED. I saved the city; nothing else can matter.

TEIR. Very well then, I shall go. Boy, take me home.

OED. Yes, let him take you. Here you are in the way,
A hindrance; out of sight is out of mind.

TEIR. I will go when my errand is done. I do not fear
Your frown. There is no way that you can harm me.
Listen to me: the man you have sought so long,

440 Threatening, issuing your proclamations
About the death of Laius—he is here,
Passing for an alien, but soon to be revealed
A Theban born; and he will find no pleasure
In this turn of fortune. He who now has eyes
Will be blind, who now is rich, a beggar,
And wander abroad with a stick to find his way.
He will be revealed as father and as brother
Of the children in his home, as son and husband
Of the woman who bore him, his father's murderer

450 And successor to his bed. Now go away
And think about these things; and if you find I lie
Then you can say that I am no true prophet.

[*Exeunt* TEIRESIAS *and* OEDIPUS]

CHORUS. Who is the man denounced
By the voice of god from the Delphian rock?
Who is the man with bloody hands
Guilty of horrors the tongue cannot name?

It is time for him to run
Faster of foot than the horses of the storm,
For the Son of Zeus is leaping upon him
With fire and lightning, and at his side   460
The Fates, remorseless avengers.

Fresh from Parnassus' snows
The call blazes forth: the hunt is up!
Search every place for the unknown man!
He doubles among the wild woods for cover,
From hole to hole in the hills,
A rogue bull running a lost race, trying
To shake off the sentence ringing in his ears
Pronounced by the shrine at earth's center, forever
Haunting him, goading him on.   470

The wise man with his birds and omens
Leaves me troubled and afraid,
Unable to believe or disbelieve.
What can I say? I fly from hope to fear.
Dark is the present, dark the days to come.
There is no quarrel that I know of
Now or in the past between
Labdacus' house and the son of Polybus,
Nothing that I could use as proof
Against Oedipus' reputation   480
In avenging Labdacus' line, and solving
The riddle of Laius' death.

To Zeus and Apollo all things are known,
They see the doings of mankind.
But who is to say that a human prophet

462 **Parnassus** mountain near Delphi celebrated as the home of
Apollo and the Muses, and also as the haunt of Dionysus

Knows any more of the future than I?
Though some men, I know, are wiser than others.
But I shall never join with his accusers
Until they have made good their charge.
490 We saw his wisdom tried and tested
When he fought the girl with wings.
Thebes took him then to her heart, and I
Will never name him guilty.

[*Enter* CREON]

CREON. Citizens, I hear that Oedipus our king
Lays monstrous charges against me, and am here
In indignation. If in the present crisis
He thinks I have injured him in any way
By word or action calculated to harm him,
I would rather die before my time is up
500 Than bear this stigma. Such malicious slander
Touches me on more than one tender spot.
What hurts me most is this—to have my friends
And you and my city brand me as a traitor.

CHORUS. This insult was probably spoken under stress,
In anger, not with deliberate intent.

CREON. And what about the taunt that the seer was coerced
Into lying by my design? Who started it?

CHORUS. It was said—I do not know how seriously.

CREON. Did he lay this charge against me steady-
510 eyed?
Did he sound as if he knew what he was saying?

CHORUS. I know nothing about it. I do not look at what

491 **the girl with wings** the Sphinx

My masters do. Here he comes himself, from the
    palace.

[*Enter* OEDIPUS]

OED. You! And what brings you here? Can you put
    on
So bold a face, to visit your victim's house,
Shown up for what you are, a murderer
Openly plotting to rob me of my crown?
In heaven's name, what did you take me for?
A fool? A coward? to entertain such schemes?
Do you think I would let you work behind my back
Unnoticed, or not take precautions once I knew?   520
Then is it not senseless, this attempt of yours
To bid for the throne alone and unsupported?
It takes men and money to make a revolution.
    CREON. Wait! You have said your say; it is now your
        turn
To listen. Learn the facts and then pass judgment.
    OED. Smooth talker! But I have no inclination
To learn from you, my bitter enemy.
    CREON. One thing let me say, before we go any
        further. . . .
    OED. One thing you must never say—that you are
        honest!   530
    CREON. If you think there is any virtue in stub-
        bornness
Devoid of reason, you have little sense.
    OED. If you think you can wrong one of your family
And get away unpunished, you are mad.
    CREON. Justly said, I grant you. But give me some
        idea,
What injury do you say that I have done you?
    OED. Did you suggest it would be advisable
To bring the prophet here, or did you not?

CREON. I did; and I am still of the same opinion.

OED. And how many years ago was it that Laius. . . .

540 CREON. That Laius what? I cannot follow you.

OED. Was lost to his people by an act of violence.

CREON. That would take us a long way back into the past.

OED. And was the prophet practicing in those days?

CREON. As skillfully as today, with equal honor.

OED. And did he then make any mention of me?

CREON. Not at any time when I was there to hear him.

OED. But did you not investigate the murder?

CREON. We were bound to, of course, but discovered nothing.

OED. And why did this know-all not tell his story then?

CREON. I prefer not to talk about things I do not
550 know.

OED. You know one thing well enough that you could tell me.

CREON. What is it? If I know, I shall keep nothing back.

OED. This: if you had not put your heads together
We should never have heard about my killing Laius.

CREON. If he says so, you know best. Now let me ask
And you must answer as I answered you.

OED. Ask what you like. I am innocent of murder.

CREON. Come now; are not you married to my sister?

OED. A question to which I can hardly answer no.
560 CREON. And you rule the country with her, equally?

OED. I give her everything that she could wish for.

CREON. Do I, the third, not rank with both of you?

OED. You do; which makes your treachery the worse.

CREON. Not if you reason with yourself as I do.
First ask yourself this question: would any man

Be king in constant fear, when he could live
In peace and quiet, and have no less power?
I want to be a king in everything
But name—and I have no desire for that,
Nor has any man who knows what is good for him.   570
As it is, I am carefree. You give me all I want,
But as king I should have many tiresome obligations.
Then why should I find monarchy more desirable
Than power and influence without the trouble?
So far I have not been misguided enough
To hanker after dishonorable gains.
As it is, all wish me well and greet me kindly,
And people with suits to you call first on me
For there are all their chances of success.
So why should I give up one life for the other?   580
No man with any sense would stoop to treason.
I have no love for such ideas, nor would I
Associate with any man who did.
Do you look for proof of this? Then go to Delphi
And ask if I quoted the oracle correctly.
And another thing; if you find that I have made
A plot with the prophet, there will be two voices
To sentence me to death—yours and my own.
But do not convict me out of mere suspicion!   590
It is hardly just to label good men bad
Or bad men good, according to your whim.
Mark my words: the man who drops an honest friend
Cuts out his heart, the thing he loves the best.
But you will learn this sure enough in time,
For time alone can tell an honest man
While one day is enough to show a villain.

    CHORUS. Good advice, my lord, for one who keeps
        a watch
For pitfalls. Hasty thoughts are dangerous.

OED. When conspirators make haste to set plots moving

600 I must make haste myself to counteract them.
If I waited and did nothing it would mean
Success for him and ruin for myself.

CREON. Then what do you want? My banishment from Thebes?

OED. No, not your banishment. I want your death!

CREON. There speaks a man who will not listen to reason.

OED. No, you must show the world what comes of envy!

CREON. I think you must be mad.

OED.   And I think sane.

CREON. Then hear me sensibly.

OED.   Hear you, a traitor?

CREON. Suppose you are wrong?

OED.   Kings must still be obeyed.

CREON. Kings, but not tyrants.

610 OED.   City, oh my city!

CREON. My city also. I have rights here too.

CHORUS. Stop this, my lords. I can see Jocasta coming
From the palace just in time. Let her advise you,
Put your quarrel aside and be friends again.

[*Enter* JOCASTA]

JOCASTA. Have you both gone out of your minds? What is the sense
Of bandying insults? Are you not ashamed
To start a private feud, when Thebes is ailing?
Come inside. And Creon, you must go back home.
Do not make a mortal grievance out of nothing.

620 CREON. Sister, your husband Oedipus thinks fit
To make me suffer one way or the other—

To drive me into banishment or kill me.

OED. Exactly. I have caught him plotting mischief—
A criminal attempt on the royal person.

CREON. May heaven's anger strike me dead this
minute

If I have done anything to deserve this charge!

JOC. In the gods' name, Oedipus, believe what he
says!

If not from respect of the oath he has sworn,

For the sake of your wife and everyone here!

CHORUS. Listen to reason, my lord;   630

I beg you, be guided by us.

OED. You ask for a favor; what is it?

CHORUS. He has been no fool in the past;

He is strong in his oath; respect him.

OED. Do you know what it is you ask?

CHORUS. I do.

OED.   Then explain yourselves; what do you
mean?

CHORUS. Your friend has invoked a curse on his
head.

Do not brand him traitor on rumor alone.

OED. You must know, by asking this

You are asking my exile or death.   640

CHORUS. No, by the Sun, the first among gods!

May I die the death that men fear most,

Shunned, unclean in the sight of heaven,

If I have such thoughts in my mind.

But my heart is heavy at our country's dying

If you add new troubles to her present load.

OED. Let him go then; but I am signing my own
death warrant

Or condemning myself to exile and disgrace.

Your voice has moved me where his oath could not.

As for him, wherever he may go, I hate him.   650

CREON. Now we have seen you—wild when you lose
　　your temper,
And yielding with bad grace. Such a nature as yours
Is its own worst enemy, and so it should be.
　　OED. Get out, and leave me in peace.
　　CREON.　　　　　　　　　　I am going.
They know I am honest, though you will not see it.

[*Exit*]

　　CHORUS. Now quickly, my lady, take him inside.
　　JOC. Not before I know what has happened.
　　CHORUS. There were words, a vague suspicion,
False, but injustice stings.
　　JOC. On both sides?
　　CHORUS.　　　　　　Yes.
660　JOC.　　　　　　　　　What was said?
　　CHORUS. Our country has troubles enough.
Better let sleeping dogs lie.
　　OED. You meant well enough, but see where it leads
　　you,
Checking me, blunting the edge of my anger.
　　CHORUS. I have said it before and say it again:
Men would think that my wits had wandered,
Would think me insane, to abandon you.
Our beloved country was sinking fast
Till you took the helm; and now you may prove
670 Our guide and salvation again.
　　JOC. Tell me as well, my lord, in heaven's name,
What can have set such fury working in you?
　　OED. I will tell you; you are more to me than they
　　are.
It is Creon, and the way he is plotting against me.
　　JOC. Go on, and tell me how this quarrel started.
　　OED. He says that I am Laius' murderer.

Joc. Does he speak from knowledge or from hearsay
   only?

OED. Neither; he sent a mischief-making prophet.
He is taking care to keep his own mouth clean.

Joc. You can relieve your mind of all such fears.   680
Listen, and learn from me: no human being
Is gifted with the art of prophecy.
Once an oracle came to Laius—I will not say
From Apollo himself, but from his ministers—
To say a child would be born to him and me
By whose hand it was fated he should die.
And Laius, as rumor goes, was killed by bandits,
From another land, at a place where three roads meet.
And as for our son, before he was in this world
Three days, Laius pinned his ankles together   690
And had him abandoned on the trackless mountain.
So in this case Apollo's purpose failed—
That the child should kill his father, or that Laius
Should be murdered by his son, the fear that haunted
   him.
So much for oracles which map our future!
Then take no notice of such things; whatever the god
Finds needful, he will show without assistance.

OED. Oh wife, the confusion that is in my heart,
The fearful apprehension, since I heard you speak!

Joc. What is it? What have I said to startle you?   700

OED. I thought I heard you telling me that Laius
Was murdered at a place where three roads meet.

Joc. Such was the story. People tell it still.

OED. What country was it where the thing was done?

Joc. In the land called Phocis, at the meeting-point
Of the roads from Delphi and from Daulia.

OED. And how many years have gone by since it
   happened?

Joc. It was just before you first appeared in Thebes

To rule us; that is when we heard of it.

OED. Oh Zeus, what have you planned to do with
710　me?

JOC. Oedipus, what is it? Why has this upset you?

OED. Do not ask me yet; but tell me about Laius.
What did he look like? How far gone in years?

JOC. A tall man, with his hair just turning gray,
To look at, not so different from you.

OED. Oh, what have I done? I think that I have laid
A dreadful curse on myself and never knew it!

JOC. What are you saying? It frightens me to look
at you.

OED. I am terrified the prophet sees too well.
720 I shall know better if you tell me one thing more.

JOC. You frighten me; but ask and I will tell you.

OED. Did he ride with a handful of men, or with a
band
Of armed retainers, as a chieftain should?

JOC. There were five in all—a herald one of them,
And a single carriage in which Laius rode.

OED. Oh, now I see it all. Jocasta, answer me,
Who was the man who told you what had happened?

JOC. A servant—the only one who returned alive.

OED. Is he with us? Is he in our household now?
730　JOC. No, he is not. When he came back and found
You ruling here in Thebes and Laius dead
He wrung me by the hand and begged me send him
Into the country where we graze our sheep
As far as possible from the sight of Thebes.
I let him go away; slave though he was
He could have asked far more and had it granted.

OED. I want him here, as fast as he can come.

JOC. That can be seen to. What is in your mind?

OED. I fear I have already said
740 More than I should; that is why I want to see him.

Joc. He shall come then; but I too have
To know what lies heavy on your heart, m
   OED. I shall keep nothing from you, n⟨
     hension
Has gone so far. Who else should I confid⟨
Unless in you, when this crisis is upon me⟨
My father's name was Polybus of Corinth,
My mother a Dorian, Merope. In that city
I lived as first in honor, till one day
There happened something—worth surprise perhaps,
But not such anger as it roused in me.   750
A man at dinner, too far gone in wine,
Jeered in his cups, I was my father's bastard.
It preyed on my mind; and I restrained myself
That day as best I could, but in the morning
Went questioning my parents. They were angry
At such a taunt, and the man who let it fly,
So on their part I was satisfied; but still
The slander rankled as it spread and grew.
And so I went, without my parents' knowledge,
On a journey to Delphi. Phoebus sent me away   760
No wiser than I came, but something else
He showed me, sad and strange and terrible:
That I was doomed to mate with my own mother,
Bring an abhorrent brood into the world;
That I should kill the father who begat me.
When I heard, I fled from Corinth, ever since
Marking its whereabouts only by the stars,
To find some place where I should never see
This evil oracle's calamities fulfilled,
And in my travels reached that very place   770
Where, as you tell me, Laius met his death.
Wife, I shall tell the truth: I was on my way

747 **Dorian** one of the oldest Greek tribes; Oedipus says this
with some pride

... had nearly come to the joining of the roads
When there met me, from the opposite direction,
A herald, and a man in a horse-drawn carriage
Exactly as you described. The fellow in front
And the old man tried to push me out of the way.
I lost my temper, hit out at the one
Who jostled me, the driver; when the old man saw it,
780 He watched me, from the carriage, coming past
And brought his double goad down on my head—
But took it back with interest! One swift blow
From the good staff in my hand, and over he went
Clean out of the chariot, sprawling on his back,
And I killed every man in sight. If this stranger
Should turn out to have anything to do with Laius,
Who is more wretched than this man before you,
And who could be more hateful to the gods,
A man no citizen, no stranger even,
790 May take into his house or speak with him
But drive him from their doors; and this, this curse
Was laid on me by no-one but myself.
And now my hands, by which he met his death,
Defile his bed. Am I not evil? Am I not
Foul through and through, when I must go to exile
And in that exile never see my people,
Or set foot in my homeland—for if I do
I must marry my mother, murder Polybus,
The father who gave me life and livelihood.
800 Then if you saw in Oedipus the prey
Of some tormenting power, would you be wrong?
Never, oh never, pure and awful gods,
Let me see that day; no, let me rather vanish
Out of the sight of men, before I see
This dreadful visitation come upon me.

    CHORUS. This is fearful, my lord; but do not give
      up hope

Until you have questioned the man who saw it done.
  OED. Yes, that is all the hope I have left me now,
To wait the coming of this man, our shepherd.
    Joc. And when he comes, what would you have from
      him?   810
  OED. I will tell you. If I find his story tallies
With yours, then it will mean that I am safe.
    Joc. And what is so important in my story?
  OED. You said that Laius, as he told the tale,
Was killed by robbers. If he stands by this,
That there were more than one, I did not kill him;
You could not make one man a company.
But if he names one solitary traveler
There is no more doubt; the deed swings back to me.
    Joc. You can be sure that this is what he said.   820
He cannot go back on it, all the city heard him.
I was not the only one. But even supposing
We find he tells a different tale today,
My lord, he can never show that Laius' death
Ran true to prophecy. Phoebus expressly said
That he was doomed to die at my child's hands;
But that unhappy babe went to his death
Before he did; then how could he have killed him?
So when it comes to oracles, after this
I shall keep both eyes fixed firmly on the front.   830
  OED. You speak good sense. But all the same, send
    someone
To bring the peasant here; do as I say.
    Joc. I will send at once. Come now, let us go home.
Would I ever fail to do anything you wanted?

[Exeunt]

  CHORUS. I pray that this may crown my every day,
In all my words and deeds to walk
Pure-hearted, in proper fear;

For thus we are commanded from on high
By laws created in the shining heavens,
840 Who know no other father but Olympus,
In their birth owing nothing to mortals
Nor sleeping though forgotten; great the god
Within them, and he grows not old.

Out of insolence is born the tyrant,
Insolence grown fat in vain
On things immoderate, unfit.
For a man who has mounted to the highest places
Must fall to meet his destiny below
Where there can be no help, no footing.
850 But honest ambition let us keep,
For thus the state is served; O Lord Apollo
Guide and strengthen me all my days.

But I pray that the man whose hands and tongue
Are arrogant, careless of retribution,
Who blasphemes in the holy places,
May fall upon evil days, the reward
Of the sin of self-conceit.
If he goes the wrong way to gain his ends,
And follows unholy courses, laying
860 Profaning hands on things he should not touch,
Could any man boast his life was safe
From the arrows of angry heaven?
But when such things as these are held in honor
Why should I sing the praises of the gods?

No longer shall I visit with my prayers
The inviolate shrine at the center of the world,

840 **Olympus** mountain home of the gods   866 **the inviolate
. . . world** Delphi; see n. on v. 70

Or. Abae's temple, or Olympia,
If the prophecy should fail to come to pass
As spoken, for all the world to see.
O Zeus, if you are rightly called   870
The Almighty, the ruler of mankind,
Look to these things; and let them not escape
Your power eternal; for the oracles
Once told of Laius are forgotten, slighted;
Apollo is divested of his glory
And man turns his face away from heaven.

[*Enter* JOCASTA]

Joc. Elders of Thebes, I have a mind to pay
A visit to the holy shrines, with gifts
Of incense and wreathed branches in my hands.
For Oedipus has let his mind succumb   880
To all manner of fears, and will not judge the present
By what has gone before, like a sensible man,
But is the prey of every fearful rumor.
There is nothing more that I can say to help him,
And so I bring offerings to you, Apollo—
The nearest to us—and request this favor:
Show us how we can find a clean way out,
For now we are afraid to see him frightened,
Like sailors who see panic in their steersman.

[*Enter* MESSENGER]

MESSENGER. Could you tell me, my friends, where
        a man might find   890
The palace of King Oedipus—better still,
Where the king himself is, if you happen to know?

867 **Abae** near Thebes, site of temple and oracle of Apollo
Olympia home of the temple of Zeus and the famous Olympic
Games   876 **and man . . . heaven** a fair description of the
growing agnosticism of Sophocles' own time

CHORUS. This is his house, and the king is indoors.
This lady is the mother of his children.

MESS. May heaven bless Oedipus' honored queen
Her whole life long with every happiness!

JOC. Stranger, I wish you the same; so fair a greeting
Deserves no less. But tell us why you come.
What have you to ask of us, or tell us?

MESS. Good news for your house, my lady, and your
900   husband!

JOC. What news is this? Who sent you here to us?

MESS. I come from Corinth; what I have to tell
Will please you, no doubt; but there is sadness too.

JOC. Pleasure and pain at once? What is this message?

MESS. The people living in the Isthmian land
Will have him for their king; so goes the story.

JOC. Why? Is old Polybus no longer king?

MESS. No, death has claimed him. He is in his grave.

JOC. What are you saying? Oedipus' father dead?

910 MESS. If I am lying, may I die myself!

JOC. Maid, run away and tell this to your master
As fast as you can. Oh gods, where are
Your oracles now? This is the man that Oedipus
Has shunned for years, for fear of killing him,
And now he is dead, and Oedipus never touched him!

[*Enter* OEDIPUS]

OED. Jocasta, dearest wife, why have you sent
For me, and called me from the palace?

JOC. Listen to this man here, and learn from his
words
To what these holy oracles have come!

920 OED. This man? Who is he? What has he to say?

905 **Isthmian land** Corinth, situated on the narrow neck of land
which joins the two parts of Greece

Joc. From Corinth; his message is that Polybus,
Your father, lives no longer—he is dead!

   Oed. What? Stranger, let me have it from your
      mouth.

   Mess. If this is where I must begin my message,
I assure you, Polybus is dead and gone.

   Oed. Did it happen by foul play? Or was he sick?

   Mess. When a man is old his life hangs by a thread.

   Oed. Poor Polybus. He died of illness, then?

   Mess. That and old age. He had lived a long life.

   Oed. Oh, wife, why should we ever spare a glance   930
For the shrine of Delphi, or the birds that scream
Above our heads? On their showing, I was doomed
To be my father's murderer; but he
Is dead and buried, and here am I, who never
Laid hand on sword. Unless perhaps he died
Through pining for me; thus I could have killed him.
But as they stand, the oracles have gone
To join him underground, and they are worthless!

   Joc. Did I not tell you so a long while since?

   Oed. You did, but I was led astray through fear.   940

   Joc. Then do not take them any more to heart.

   Oed. But my mother's bed . . . how should I not
      fear that?

   Joc. What has a man to fear, when life is ruled
By chance, and the future is unknowable?
The best way is to take life as it comes.
So have no fear of marriage with your mother.
Many men before this time have dreamt that they
Have shared their mother's bed. The man to whom
These things are nothing lives the easiest life.

   Oed. It would be well enough to talk in such a way 950
If my mother were not living. As she is,
Though your words make sense, I have good cause to
      fear.

Joc. But your father's death is a ray of light in darkness.

Oed. A bright one; but I fear the living woman.

Mess. Who is this woman that you are afraid of?

Oed. Merope, old man, the wife of Polybus.

Mess. And what is there in her to make you afraid?

Oed. A terrifying oracle from heaven.

Mess. May it be told? Or are you sworn to silence?

960 Oed. Why should it not? Apollo told me once

That I was doomed to marry with my mother

And shed my father's blood with these my hands.

And that is why I put my home in Corinth

Behind me—for the best, but all the same

There is nothing so sweet as the sight of parents' faces.

Mess. Was it for fear of this you left our city?

Oed. It was; and to avoid my father's murder.

Mess. Then had I better not remove your fear,

My lord, since I am here with friendly purpose?

970 Oed. If so you would deserve reward, and have it.

Mess. Indeed, this was my principal reason for coming,

To do myself some good when you came home.

Oed. I shall never come. I must not see my parents.

Mess. My son, I see you are making a mistake—

Oed. What do you mean, old man? In god's name
tell me.

Mess. —if you shrink from going home because of
this.

Oed. I am terrified of proving Phoebus true.

Mess. Of the guilt and shame that will come to you
through your parents?

Oed. You have it, old man; that fear is always with
me.

Mess. Then let me tell you that these fears are
980   groundless!

OED. How can they be, if I were born their son?

MESS. Because there is none of Polybus' blood in you.

OED. Are you telling me that he was not my father?

MESS. No more than I—one thing we had in common.

OED. What could he have in common with a nobody?

MESS. Why, I am not your father, and neither was he.

OED. But then . . . he called me son . . . what made him do it?

MESS. He took you as a present from my hands.

OED. He had such love . . . for an adopted son?

MESS. He had no sons of his own; this moved his heart. 990

OED. You gave me to him—had you bought me? Found me?

MESS. I found you, in the wild woods of Cithairon.

OED. What led your wanderings to such a place?

MESS. I was in charge of sheep there, on the mountain.

OED. A shepherd, going from place to place for hire?

MESS. But your preserver at that time, my son.

OED. Why? What was matter with me when you found me?

MESS. Your ankles are best witnesses of that.

OED. Oh, why do you have to talk of that old trouble?

MESS. They were pinned together, and I cut you loose. 1000

OED. A shameful mark I carried from my cradle.

MESS. And from this chance you took the name you bear.

OED. Who did this to me? My father or my mother?

MESS. The man who gave you me knows; I do not.

OED. You took me from someone else? You did not
find me?

MESS. No, another shepherd passed you on to me.

OED. Who was this man? Can you identify him?

MESS. We knew him, I think, as one of Laius' people.

OED. You mean the king who used to rule this
country?

MESS. The very same. This man was Laius' herds-
1010   man.

OED. And is he still alive for me to see him?

MESS. You in this country would best know of that.

OED. My people, is there anyone here present

Who knows the herdsman he is talking of,

Who has seen him in the country or the town?

Come, tell me; it is time to solve this riddle.

CHORUS. I think he means no other than the man

You already want to see. Jocasta here

Would be best qualified to tell you that.

1020   OED. My lady, do you know the man we mean—

The man we just sent for; is he speaking of him?

JOC. Why ask who he means? Do not bother with it.

This story is not worth thinking of; it is nothing.

OED. No, that can never be. I have the clues

Here in my hand. I must find out my birth.

JOC. No, by the gods! If you care for your own
safety

Ask no more questions. I have suffered enough.

OED. Take courage. If my mother was a slave, and
hers,

And hers before her, you are still pure-born.

1030   JOC. Listen, please listen to me! Do not do this!

OED. No-one could stop me finding out the truth.

JOC. It is for your sake; I advise you for the best.

OED. If this is your best, I have no patience with it.

JOC. I pray you may never find out who you are.

OED. Go, somebody, and fetch the herdsman here.
Leave her to glory in her wealthy birth!
    JOC. Accursed! Accursed! I have no other name
To call you; you will never hear me again.

[*Exit*]

    CHORUS. What can have made her leave you, Oedi-
        pus,
In this burst of frantic grief? I have a fear   1040
That from her silence there will break a storm.
    OED. Let break what will! As for my parentage,
Humble though it may be, I want to know it.
She is a woman, with a woman's pride,
And is ashamed, no doubt, of my low birth.
But I proclaim myself the child of Luck,
My benefactress; this is no dishonor.
Yes, Luck is my mother, and the months, my cousins,
Saw me first humble and then saw me great.
With such a parentage I could not be false   1050
To myself again, or let this secret rest.
    CHORUS. If I am any judge of the future,
If my mind does not play me false,
Cithairon, tomorrow at the full moon's rising,
By Olympus, you will need no second telling
That Oedipus boasts of your kinship, hailing you
As nurse and mother.
And we shall be there with dances in your honor
Because you have found favor in our king's sight.
Apollo, hear us when we pray,   1060
And bless our good intentions!

Which of the nymphs, the long-lived ones,
Lay with the mountain-wanderer Pan

1063 **Pan** primitive nature deity, half man, half goat

To bring you to birth? Or was it Loxias?
He is a god who loves the upland pastures.
Or was it Cyllene's lord, or the god
Of the Bacchanals, dwelling
High in the hilltops, who received you,
A new-born treasure, from the arms of a nymph
1070 Of Helicon, the favorite
Companions of his pleasure?

[*Enter attendants with* HERDSMAN]

OED. Elders, if I, who never saw the man,
May make a guess, I think I see the herdsman
We have sought so long; he is well advanced in years—
This answers the description—and besides
I recognize the men escorting him
As servants of my own. But you may well
Have the advantage of me, if you have seen him before;
CHORUS. I know him, no mistake. He worked for Laius,
1080 As honest a shepherd as you could hope to find.
OED. First let me hear from you, my Corinthian friend.
Is this your man?
MESS. The one you see before you.
OED. Come here, old man, and look me in the face.
Answer my questions. You once worked for Laius?
HERDSMAN. I did; and I was palace-bred, not bought.
OED. In what employment? How did you spend your time?

1064 **Loxias** Apollo   1066 **Cyllene's lord** Hermes, the messenger god, born on Mount Cyllene   1067 **Bacchanals** frenzied women who worshipped Dionysus   1070 **Helicon** mountain sacred to Apollo and the Muses

HERDS. For the best part of my life I watched the
flocks.

OED. What part of the country did you mostly work
in?

HERDS. Sometimes Cithairon, sometimes round about.

OED. Have you seen this man in those parts, to your
knowledge?   1090

HERDS. Who? Doing what? What man are you talking about?

OED. This man in front of you. Have you ever met
him?

HERDS. Not to remember off-hand. I cannot say.

MESS. Small wonder, master. But let me refresh
His failing memory. I have no doubt
That he recalls the time we spent together
In the country round Cithairon. He had two flocks,
And I, his mate, had one. Three years we did this,
For six months at a time, from spring to fall.
Then, for the winter, I used to drive my flocks   1100
Home to my fold, he his to that of Laius.
Did it happen as I say, or did it not?

HERDS. Yes, true; but it was many years ago.

MESS. Now tell me: do you remember giving me
A boy for me to bring up as my own?

HERDS. What now? What has put that question in
your head?

MESS. That child, my friend, is the man you see
before you.

HERDS. Curse you! Do not say another word!

OED. Old man, do not reprove him. Your words
stand
In greater need of admonition than his.   1110

HERDS. And where do I offend, most noble master?

OED. In not telling of the boy he asks about.

HERDS. This meddler does not know what he is saying.

OED. If you will not speak to oblige me I must make you.

HERDS. No, no, for god's sake; you would not hurt an old man?

OED. Quickly, somebody, tie his arms behind him.

HERDS. Unhappy man, what more do you want to know?

OED. This child he talks of; did you give it him?

HERDS. I did; and I wish that day had been my last

1120 OED. It will come to that, unless you tell the truth.

HERDS. I shall do myself more harm by telling you.

OED. It seems he is determined to waste our time.

HERDS. No, no! I told you once, I gave it him.

OED. Where did you get it? Your home or another's?

HERDS. It was not mine. Somebody gave it me.

OED. Who? Which one of my people? Where does he live?

HERDS. No, master, in heaven's name, ask no more questions.

OED. You are a dead man if I have to ask again.

HERDS. It was a child of the house of Laius.

1130 OED. A slave? Or one of his own family?

HERDS. I am near to saying what should not be said.

OED. And I to hearing; but it must be heard.

HERDS. They said it was Laius' son. But go inside
And ask your wife; for she could tell you all.

OED. You mean she gave it you?

HERDS.   She did, my lord.

OED. But why?

HERDS.   For me to make away with it.

OED. Her child!

HERDS.   She feared an evil prophecy.

OED. What was it?

HERDS.   That the son should kill his father.

OED. Then why did you give him up to this old man?

HERDS. For pity, master, thinking he would take   1149
The child home, out of Thebes; but he preserved him
For a fate worse than any other. If you are truly
The man he says, then know you were born accursed.

[Exit]

OED. Oh, oh, then everything has come out true.
Light, I shall not look on you again.
I have been born where I should not be born,
I have married where I should not marry,
I have killed whom I should not kill; now all is clear.

[Exit]

CHORUS. You that are born into this world,
I count you in your lives as nothing worth.   1150
What man has ever won for himself
More of happiness than this,
To seem, and having seemed, to pass?
For Oedipus, when I look at you
And the fate which fell upon you, can I
Call any human being happy?

Zeus knows, his arrow went straight to its mark
And all of life's blessings became his prize.
He killed the girl with the crooked claws,
The riddle-monger, and stood up among us   1160
A tower of strength to drive death from our land,
For which we called you our king, ᵖ
The greatest we knew; in the proud
Of Thebes you were lord and mast

Now who has a sadder tale to tell?
A life turned upside down,

The door flung wide to misfortune,
The hounds of fate let loose.
Oh Oedipus, famous Oedipus,
1170 The same ample shelter sufficed
For father and son, a bed for the mating.
How could the furrows your father sowed
Have endured you so long in silence?

Time sees all, and has found you out
Despite yourself, passing sentence
On the marriage that is no marriage,
Where begetter is one with begotten.
Laius' child, oh Laius' child,
Better if I had not seen you,
1180 For when all is said, he that gave me new life
Has taken all my joy in living.

[*Enter* SECOND MESSENGER]

MESS. Ancestral and most honorable lords,
Such things you will see and hear of; such a weight
Of grief is yours, if like true sons of Thebes
You still care for the sons of Labdacus.
I think there is no river wide enough
To wash this palace clean, so many are
The horrors it hides, or soon will bring to light,
Done willfully, from choice; no sufferengs
1190 Hurt more than those we bring upon ourselves.
CHORUS. Those that we know already claim their
weight
Of tears. What more have you to add to these?
MESS. A tale which can be very briefly told
And heard: our royal lady Jocasta is dead.
CHORUS. Oh miserable queen; what was the cause?
MESS. By her own hand. The worst of what has hap-
pened

You shall be spared, you were not there to see it.
But you shall hear as much as I recall
About the sufferings of the wretched queen.
Past caring what she did, she rushed inside   1200
The hall, and made straight for her marriage bed,
Head in hands, and fingers tearing at her hair.
Once in the room she slammed the doors behind her
And called on Laius rotting in his grave,
Remembering a once begotten child
By whom the father should die, and leave the mother
To bear his son's cursed children; she bewailed
The bed where she had borne a double brood,
Husband by husband, children by her child,
And then she died—I cannot tell you how,   1210
For Oedipus burst on us with a cry
And we had no chance to watch her agonies.
We had eyes for none but him, as he ran from one
To another, demanding a sword, and where
He might find his wife—his mother, not his wife,
The womb that gave him and his children birth.
In his frenzy he was guided by some power
More than human—not by any of us who stood there.
With a dreadful cry, as though a hand had pointed,
He sprang at the double doors, forced back the bolts 1220
Till the sockets gave, and ran into the room.
And there inside we saw the woman hanging,
Her body swinging in a twist of rope.
When he saw, a shuddering cry welled up inside him;
He cut the noose that held her; when she lay
Cold on the ground, we saw a ghastly sight.
He tore away the golden brooches from
Her dress, that she had used as ornaments,
And lifted them, and plunged them in his eyes   1230
With words like these: "You shall not see again

Such horrors as I did, saw done to me,
But stare in darkness on forbidden faces,
Meet those I longed to find, and pass them by."
And to this tune he raised his hands and struck
His eyes again and again; with every blow
Blood spurted down his cheeks. It did not fall
In slow and sluggish drops, but all at once
Black blood came pouring like a shower of hail.
This storm has broken on two people's heads,
1240 Not one alone; both man and wife have suffered.
Till now, the happiness they inherited
Was happiness indeed; and now, today,
Tears, ruin, death, disgrace, as many ills
As there are names for them; not one is lacking.

    CHORUS. How is he now? Is he in peace from pain?
    MESS. He shouts for the doors to be opened, for
      every man
In Thebes to see his father's murderer,
His mother's—heaven forbid I speak that word.
He means to cast himself from Thebes, to stay
1250 In this house no more, a self-inflicted curse.
But his strength is gone; he needs someone to guide
His steps, the pain is more than he can bear.
And this too he will show you. See, the doors
Are opening, and soon you will see a sight
To move your tears, though you recoil from it.

[*Enter* OEDIPUS, *blind*]

    CHORUS. Oh sufferings dreadful to see,
Most dreadful of all that ever
Greeted my eyes. Wretched king,
What insanity possessed you?
1260 What demon, in one colossal spring
Pounced on your ill-fated life?

Unhappy king,
I cannot even look you in the face,
Though there are still many questions to be asked,
Many things left unsaid, much remaining to be seen,
You fill me with such shuddering.

    OED. Oh, oh, the pain, the pain!
Where do my poor legs take me?
Where do the wild winds scatter my words?
Oh, my fate, where have you leapt with me?   1270

    CHORUS. To a dreadful place that must not be
      named,
To a place unfit for the eyes of man.

    OED. Oh, this fog,
This horrible darkness all around me,
Unspeakable visitation
Blown by an evil wind; I am powerless.
Oh, when I remember my sorrows
I feel again the points in my eyes.

    CHORUS. No wonder; in such sorrows you must have
Evils redoubled to endure and mourn.   1280

    OED. Oh, my friend,
You are my faithful servant still,
Blind Oedipus' patient nurse.
I know you are here, I can feel your presence.
Although I am in the darkness
I can recognize your voice.

    CHORUS. Oh man of wrath, how could you bring
      yourself
To blind your eyes? What demon drove you on?

    OED. It was Apollo, my friends, Apollo
Who contrived my ruin, who worked my fall.
But no-one blinded my eyes
But myself, in my own grief.
What use are eyes to me, who could
See anything pleasant again?

CHORUS. Yes, it was as you say.

OED. What is there left for me to see,
To love? Who still has a kindly word
My friends, for me?
Take me away from this land, my friends,·
1300 Take me with all the speed you may,
For Oedipus is no more,
Contaminated, cursed,
Unclean in heaven's sight.

CHORUS. Knowledge and pain; they hurt you equally.
I wish your path and mine had never crossed.

OED. Cursed be the man who struck the cruel chains
From my feet as I lay abandoned,
And saved me from death, gave me back
To the world of the living—why?
1310 If I had died then, I should never
Have grieved myself or my loved ones so.

CHORUS. I too would have had it so.

OED. I would not have shed my father's blood
Or heard men call me my mother's husband.
And now I am
God-shunned, the son of a mother defiled,
Have taken my turn in my mother's bed.
If there is any sorrow
Greater than all others
1320 It belongs to Oedipus.

CHORUS. I cannot praise your judgment. You would
be
Far better dead than living still and blind.

OED. Do not tell me I am wrong. What I have done
Is best as it is. Give me no more advice.
If I had sight, I know not with what eyes
I would have looked upon my father, when
I walked among the dead, or my sad mother,
For sins so great cannot be paid by hanging.

Or do you think the sight of children born
As mine were born could give me any joy?   1330
No, never to these eyes of mine again,
Nor the proud wall of our city, nor the holy
Statues of our gods; these I, ten times accursed,
I, who was noblest of the sons of Thebes,
Have set behind me by my own command
That all cast out the sinner, the man revealed
By heaven as unclean, as Laius' son.
And tainted thus for all the world to see
How could I look my people in the face?
I could not. If I could have stopped my ears,   1340
My fount of hearing, I would not have rested
Till I had made a prison of this body
Barred against sight and sound. How happy the mind
That can so live, beyond the reach of suffering.
Cithairon, why did you shelter me? Why did you not
Kill me there, where you found me, so that I might
     never
Show to mankind the secret of my birth?
Oh Polybus, Corinth, the ancestral home
Men called my father's; oh, how fair of face
Was I, your child, and how corrupt beneath!   1350
For now I am found evil, evil born.
Those three roads, and the hidden clump of trees,
The wood, the narrow place where three paths met,
Who drank from my own hands the father's blood,
And so, my own blood; do you still remember
The things you saw me do? Then I came here
To do other things besides. Oh marriage, marriage,
You gave me birth, and after I was born
Bore children to your child, and brought to light
Sons, fathers, brothers in a web of incest,   1360
Than which men know nothing more abominable.
But what is sin to do is sin to speak of.

For heaven's love, hide me in some wilderness,
Or strike me dead, or throw me in the sea,
Where you will never set eyes on me again.
Come, do not shrink from touching my poor body.
Please; do not be afraid. My sufferings
Are all my own, no-one will be infected.

    CHORUS. No. Here is Creon, in time to listen to you,
1370 Ready to act or advise. Now you are gone
He is the only one we have to turn to.

    OED. Oh, what words can I find to say to him?
What proof of my good faith? I have been found
An arrant traitor to him in the past.

[*Enter* CREON *with attendants*]

    CREON. Oedipus, I have not come to jeer at you
Or throw your past misconduct in your face.

[*To the* CHORUS]

As for you, if you have no sense of decency
To a fellow man, at least have some respect
For holy sunlight, giver of warmth and life.
1380 Do not leave this pollution uncovered, an offence
To earth, to light, to the pure rain from heaven.
Take him indoors as quickly as you can.
Propriety forbids he should be made
A public spectacle. These things are for his family.

    OED. Listen: since you have removed my apprehension
And behave so nobly to a man so low
Grant me this favor—for your good, not for mine.

    CREON. What is it you are so anxious to have me do?

    OED. Lose no more time; drive me away from Thebes
1390 To some place where nobody will know my name.

    CREON. Believe me, I would have done so; but first
I wanted

To find out from the god what I should do.

OED. The will of god is clear enough already.

Kill the parricide, the sinner; and that am I.

CREON. So he said. But all the same, now things
have gone

So far, it is better that we seek clear guidance.

OED. You will go to the god? For a poor wretch like
myself?

CREON. I will. Perhaps you will believe him this
time.

OED. I do. And I will urge your duties on you.

The woman inside—bury her as you would wish   1400

To be buried yourself. It is right, she is your sister.

But as for me, never sentence my father's city

To have me within its walls, as long as I live,

But leave me to the hills, to my Cithairon

As men now call it—destined for my grave

By my father and mother when they were alive.

They tried to kill me; let me die the way they wanted.

But I am sure of one thing; no disease,

Nothing can kill me now. I would not have been saved

From death, unless it were for some strange destiny. 1410

But let my destiny go where it will.

As for my children—Creon, do not trouble yourself

About my sons. They are men, they can never lack

A livelihood, wherever they may be.

But my two girls, my poor unhappy daughters,

Who never knew what it was to eat a meal

Away from their father's side, but had their share

Of every little thing I had myself. . . .

Please look after them. And I beg this favor now,   1420

Let me lay my hands on them and weep with them.

Please, my lord,

Please, noble heart. If I could touch them now

I should think they were with me, as if I could see
  them.

[*Enter* ANTIGONE *and* ISMENE]

What is that?
Oh you gods; is it my darlings that I hear
Sobbing? Has Creon taken pity on me
And sent my darlings, sent my children to me?
Am I right?

　　CREON. Yes, I had them brought to you; I knew
1430 They would delight you as they always have done.

　　OED. Bless you for your trouble. May you find
A kinder fate than what has come to me.
Where are you now, my children? Over here:
Come to these hands of mine, your brother's hands,
Whose offices have made your father's eyes
That were once so bright, to see as they see now.
For the truth is out; your father, stupid, blind,
Begot you in the womb where he was born.
Sight have I none, but tears I have for you
1440 When I think of how you will be forced to live
At men's hands in the bitter days to come.
What gathering of the folk will you attend,
What festival that will not send you home
In tears, instead of making holiday?
And when the time has come for you to marry,
Show me the man, my children, bold enough
To take upon his own head such disgrace,
The stain that you and your brothers will inherit.
What sorrow is not ours? Your father killed
1450 His father, sowed his seed in her
Where he was sown as seed, and did beget you
In the selfsame place where he was once begotten.
That is how men will talk. Then who will marry you?
No-one, my children. Marriage is not for you.

You must be barren till your lives are done.
Son of Menoeceus, you are the only father
These girls have left, for we, their parents,
Are both of us gone. So do not let them wander
Beggared and husbandless. They are your kin.
And do not level them with my misfortunes   1460
But pity them. You see how young they are.
You are the only friend they have in the world.
Touch me, kind heart, in token of your promise.
Children, if you were old enough to understand,
There is much I could say to help you. As it is,
Pray after me—to live with moderation
And better fortune than your father did.

CREON. Your time is up. Dry your tears and go indoors.

OED. It is hard, but I must obey.

CREON.   There must be moderation in all things.

OED. I shall go on one condition.

CREON.   Tell me what it is.   1470

OED. Send me away from Thebes to live.

CREON.   That is for the gods to say.

OED. They will be glad to see me gone.

CREON.   Then your wish will soon be granted.

OED. You agree then?

CREON.   When I do not know, I do not speak.

OED. Take me away, it is time.

CREON.   Come along. Leave your children here.

OED. Never part us!

CREON.   Do not ask to have everything your way.
Your time for giving orders is over.

[*Exeunt*]

CHORUS. People of this city, look, this pus,
Who guessed the famous riddle, who rose

Envy of all in the city who saw his good fortune.
And now what a fearful storm of disaster has struck
1480   him.
That is why we wait until we see the final day,
Not calling anybody happy who is mortal
Until he has passed the last milestone without ca-
    lamity.

ANTIGONE

DRAMATIS PERSONAE

ANTIGONE, daughter of dead King Oedipus
ISMENE, her sister
CHORUS of Theban elders
CREON, uncle of ANTIGONE and ISMENE, King of Thebes
GUARD
HAEMON, son of CREON, betrothed to ANTIGONE
TEIRESIAS, a blind prophet
FIRST MESSENGER
EURYDICE, wife of CREON
SECOND MESSENGER

Guards and Attendants

SCENE: Before the palace of CREON in Thebes

ANTIGONE

[*Enter* ANTIGONE *and* ISMENE]

ANTIGONE. Ismene, my dear, my mother's child, my
    sister,
What part of Oedipus' sad legacy
Has Zeus not laid in full on us who live?
There is nothing bitter, nothing of disaster,
No shame, no humiliation I have not seen
In the number of your sufferings and mine.
And now what is this order which they say
Our leader has announced throughout the city?
Do you know? Have you heard? Or do I have to tell
    you
That what has happened to our enemies   **10**
Is threatening to fall upon our friends?

    ISMENE. I have heard no word of friends, Antigone,
To bring me comfort or to bring me pain
Since the time we two were robbed of our two
    brothers,
Dead in one day, and by each other's hand.
And now the Argive army overnight
Has disappeared, I am no nearer knowing
Whether my luck has changed for good or bad.

10 That what . . . friends? the bodies of the warriors of Argos,
who had aided Polyneices in his attempt on Thebes, had been
left unburied; this punishment is now to be extended to Polyneices himself, although a Theban born

ANT. I know, too well. That is why I wanted to
    bring you
20 Outside the courtyard, to talk to you alone.
    ISM. What is it? Trouble, you do not need to tell me.
    ANT. What else, when Creon singles out one brother
For a hero's grave, and lets the other rot?
They are saying he has laid Eteocles in the ground
With every rite and custom that is fitting
To give him honor with the dead below.
But Polyneices' body, that was killed
So pitifully, they say he has commanded
Should not be mourned or given burial
30 But lie unburied and unwept, a feast
For passing birds to gorge on at their pleasure.
And so, the rumor runs, has our good Creon
Decreed for you and me—for me, I say!
And is on his way here now, to spell it out
To those who have not heard. He does not take
This matter lightly. Anyone who disobeys
In any way will die by public stoning.
So there you have it. Now we shall soon find out
If you are a true-born daughter of your line,
40 Or if you will disgrace your noble blood!
    ISM. But, my poor sister, if things are as you say,
What ways and means have I to set them straight?
    ANT. Ask yourself, will you work with me, help
    me do it?
    ISM. What adventure is this? What do you have in
    mind?
    ANT. Will you help this hand of mine to lift the
    dead?
    ISM. You mean to bury him? Against the law?
    ANT. Bury my brother? Yes—and bury yours,
If you will not. No-one shall call me faithless.

Ism. You would not dare, when Creon has forbidden
　　it!

Ant. He has no right to keep me from my own.　　50
　　Ism. Oh sister, think of how our father died,
Hated, despised, and driven by the sins
He had himself laid bare, to turn his hand
Against himself, and strike out both his eyes.
And then his mother, wife—which shall I call her?
Knotted a noose, and took away her life.
Then the final blow, two brothers in one day,
Unhappy pair, each shedding kinsman's blood,
Lay hands on each other, and made one in death.
Now we two are alone. Think how much worse　　60
Our deaths will be, if in despite of law
We brave the king's commandment and his power.
Let us not forget two things—that we were born
Women, and so not meant to fight with men;
And then, that we must do what our masters tell us—
Obey in this, and other things far worse.
I, then, will ask the kingdom of the dead
To pardon me; since I am no free agent,
I will yield to the powers that be. There is no sense
In meddling in things outside our sphere.　　70
　　Ant. I shall not persuade you. You would not be
　　welcome
To help me now, even if you wanted to.
Be what you want to be; but I intend
To bury him. It is a noble way to die.
I shall lie with him for love, as he loved me,
A criminal, but guiltless; for the dead
Have longer claims upon me than the living.
There is my lasting home. If you think fit
To dishonor the gods' commandments, then you may.
　　Ism. I mean them no dishonor; but when it means　　80
Defying the state—I am not strong enough.

Ant. Let that be your excuse. Now I shall go
To heap the earth on my beloved brother.

Ism. Antigone, no! I am so afraid for you!

Ant. You need not fear for me. Look after yourself.

Ism. At least tell no-one what you mean to do.
Keep it a secret, I shall do the same.

Ant. Oh no, denounce me! You will be in far worse
trouble
For keeping silence, if you do not tell the world.

Ism. You have a hot heart where you should be shiv-
90   ering.

Ant. I know I am giving pleasure where I should.

Ism. Yes, if you can. But you ask too much of yourself.

Ant. When I have no more strength, then I shall
stop.

Ism. No point in starting, when the cause is hopeless.

Ant. Go on like this and you will make me hate you,
And the dead will hate you too; you give him cause.
Leave me alone with my stupidity
To face this dread unknown; whatever it is,
Anything is better than to die a coward!

Ism. Then if your mind is made up, go. You are a
100   fool,
And yet your own will love you for it.

[*Exit* Antigone; Ismene *retires within the palace.
Enter* Chorus *of Theban elders.*]

Chorus. Light of the morning sun, brightest that
ever yet
Dawned upon the seven gates of Thebes;
Eye of the golden day, at last we see you
Rising over Dirke's streams,

105 **Dirke** river on the west of Thebes

Turning to rout the white-shielded warrior
That came from Argos in his array,
Winging his feet, and sending him flying home.

Polyneices' contentious quarrel
Was the cause of his coming here,   110
Winging over our country
Like an eagle clamoring,
Sheathed in snow-white feathers
With mail-clad men and waving plumes.

Over the housetops hovering, howling before
Our seven gates for blood to slake his spears;
But before he could suck his fill of Theban
Blood, before the Fire-god's flame
Leapt from the logs to embrace our ramparts,
He left, so loud the roaring of the war-cry   120
Behind him, as he fought the Theban dragon.

Zeus hates nothing more than a boastful tongue.
When he saw them coming, a mighty stream
Arrogant in their clanging gold
He brandished his thunderbolt and felled the man
Who had scaled our ramparts, and stood at his goal
With the cry of victory on his lips.

And over he tumbled, torch in hand,
He who a moment before
Had come at us like a man possessed,   130
Running berserk, with the hot breath of hatred.
Earth rang with his fall, and his threats went wide.

125 **the man . . . ramparts** a famous incident in the Theban
story. Capaneus, one of the seven heroes who marched against
the city, dared to defy Zeus and for his presumption was struck
down at the moment of his triumph

Then the God of War, our good yoke-fellow,
Lashed out, and assigned
To each of the rest their several deaths.

Seven captains stood before seven gates,
Matched against seven, and left their armor
In homage to Zeus, the arbiter of battles,
All but the ill-starred pair, who, born
140 Of one father and mother, leveled their spears
At each other; both won, and both fell dead.

But now the glorious name of Victory
Enters our chariot-proud
City, to laugh with us in our joy,
Let us put all memory of past war behind us
And visit the temples of the gods with song
And with nightlong dances; Bacchus, whose steps
Set the meadows dancing,
Come down to lead the procession!

[*Enter* CREON]

150 But here comes our country's ruler,
Creon, Menoeceus' son, our new lord
By the gods' new dispensations.
What counsel can he be pondering
To summon the elders by general decree
To meet in special conference together?
  CREON. Gentlemen, the state has been in troubled
    waters,
But now the gods have set us back on course.
My summons came to you, of all the people,
To meet here privately, because I knew
160 Your constant reverence for Laius' throne,
And then, when Oedipus became our king,
After his death, I saw their children

Secure in your unswerving loyalty.
And now this double blow has taken both
His sons in one day, each struck down by the other,
Each with his brother's blood upon his hands,
The throne and all its powers come to me
As next of kin in order of succession.
But you can never know what a man is made of,
His character or powers of intellect,   170
Until you have seen him tried in rule and office.
A man who holds the reins of government
And does not follow the wisest policies
But lets something scare him from saying what he
      thinks,
I hold despicable, and always have done.
Nor have I time for anyone who puts
His popularity before his country.
As Zeus the omnipotent will be my witness,
If I saw our welfare threatened; if I saw
One danger-signal, I would speak my mind,   180
And never count an enemy of my country
To be a friend of mine. This I believe:
The state keeps us afloat. While she holds an even keel,
Then, and then only, can we make real friends.
By this creed I shall make Thebes prosperous;
And in accordance with it, I have published
My edict on the sons of Oedipus,
That Eteocles, who died a hero's death
While fighting to defend his fatherland
Should be entombed with every solemn rite   190
With which the glorious dead are sent to rest.
But his brother Polyneices, who returned
From exile, with intent to devastate
The country of his fathers, and to burn
The temples of his fathers' gods, to taste
His brother's blood, and make the rest his slaves,

Concerning him, it is proclaimed as follows:
That nobody shall mourn or bury him,
But let his body lie for dogs and birds
200 To make their meal, so men may look and shudder.
Such is my policy; foul play shall never
Triumph over honest merit, if I can help it,
But the man who loves his city shall receive
Honor from me, in his life and in his death.

    CHORUS. Such is your pleasure, Creon, son of Menoe-
      ceus,
Concerning our city's friend and enemy,
And you have the power to order as you wish,
Not only the dead, but the living too.

    CREON. Then see to it my orders are obeyed.
210   CHORUS. Lay this responsibility on someone younger!
    CREON. No, not to guard the corpse; that has been
      seen to.
    CHORUS. Then what else are you asking me to do?
    CREON. Not to side with anyone who disobeys me.
    CHORUS. No man is fool enough to ask for death.
    CREON. That is what you would get. But hope of gain
Has often led men on to their destruction.

[*Enter* GUARD]

    GUARD. My lord, I won't say that I'm out of breath
From hurrying, or that I've run here all the way,
For several times my thoughts pulled me up short
220 And made me turn round to go back again.
There was a voice inside me kept on saying
"Why go, you fool? You're certain to be punished."
"Idiot, why hang about? If Creon hears
The news from someone else, you'll smart for it."
Arguing like this I went at snail's pace,
And so a short road turned into a long one.
But in the end, go forward won the day.

There's nothing to say, but all the same I'll say it.
I'm certain of one thing, at any rate,
That I can only get what's coming to me.   230
    CREON. What is it that has put such fear in you?
    GUARD. First let me say a word on my own account.
I didn't do it, nor did I see who did,
And it isn't right that I should take the blame for it.
    CREON. A well-placed shot. You have covered your-
      self
Well against attack. I see you mean to surprise me.
    GUARD. A man thinks twice before he tells bad news.
    CREON. Then tell me, will you, and be on your way.
    GUARD. Well, here it is: the corpse—someone has
      buried it.
And gone away; he sprinkled dry dust over   240
The flesh, and did whatever else was fitting.
    CREON. What are you saying? What man has dared
      to do this?
    GUARD. I don't know. There was no mark of a pick-
      axe,
No spade had been at work; the ground was hard,
Dry and unbroken; we could find no tracks
Of wheels; he left no trace, whoever did it.
And when the man who took the morning watch
Showed us, nobody knew what to make of it.
The corpse was out of sight—not in a tomb
But sprinkled with dust, as though someone had thrown
    it   250
To avoid bad luck. There was no sign of wild beasts
Or dogs around; the corpse was in one piece.
Then we all started cursing each other at once,
One sentry blaming the next; it would have come
To blows in the end, there was no-one there to stop us.
First one had done it, then the next man, then the next,
But we couldn't pin it down, all pleaded ignorance.

We were ready to take red-hot irons in our hands,
To walk through fire, to swear an oath to heaven
260 That we were innocent, had no idea
Of who had planned it all, or done the work.
In the end, when there was no more point in searching,
One man said something which made every one of us
Shiver, and hang our heads; we didn't see
How we could argue with him, or if we listened
How we could save our necks. He said we couldn't
Keep the thing dark, but we must come and tell you.
So we did; and I was the unlucky one.
The lot picked me to receive the prize.
270 So here I am—about as pleased to be here
As I know you are to see me. Nobody
Has any love for the one who brings bad news.

   CHORUS. My lord, since he began, I have been won-
      dering
Could this perhaps have been the work of heaven?

    CREON. Be quiet, before you make me lose my tem-
      per.
Do you want to look like fools in your old age?
What you suggest is intolerable,
That the gods would give this corpse a second thought.
Why should they try to hide his nakedness?
280 In reward for services rendered? When he came
To burn their marble halls and treasuries,
To burn their land, make havoc of its laws?
Or can you see the gods rewarding sinners?
Never. No, there were people in this town
Who took it hard from the first, and grumbled at me,
Furtively tossing their heads, not submitting
To the yoke as in duty bound, like contented men.
It was these people—of that I am convinced—
Who bribed the guards and urged them on to do it.
290 Of all the institutions of mankind

The greatest curse is money. It destroys
Our cities, it takes men away from home,
Corrupts men's honest minds, and teaches them
To enter on disreputable courses.
It shows them how to lead immoral lives
And flout the gods in everything they do.
But every one of the bribers will be caught
Sooner or later, they may be sure of that.
But by the reverence I owe to Zeus,
I tell you this upon my solemn oath,   300
That if you do not find the author of
This burial, and produce him before my eyes,
Death alone will be too good for you; you will be
Left hanging, till you tell about this outrage.
Then, when you next go stealing, you will know
What you may take, and learn for once and all
Not to love money without asking where
It comes from. You will find ill-gotten gains
Have ruined many more than they have saved.

GUARD. May I speak? Or shall I just turn round and
go?   310

CREON. Do you still need telling that your voice an-
noys me?

GUARD. Where does it hurt? In your ears or in your
heart?

CREON. Is there any call for you to define my pain?

GUARD. The criminal troubles your mind, and I your
ears.

CREON. Oh, you were born with a loose tongue, I can
see.

GUARD. Maybe I was, but this I didn't do.

CREON. You did, and worse. You sold your life for
money.

GUARD. How dreadful to judge by appearances, then
be wrong.

CREON. Moralize as you please; but if you do not
show me
320 The men who did this thing, you will bear witness
That dishonest winnings bring you into trouble.

[*Exit* CREON *to the palace*]

GUARD. Well, I only hope he's caught; but whether
he is
Or not—it's in the hands of fortune now—
You won't see me coming this way again.
I never thought I'd get away with this.
It's more than I hoped—the gods be praised for it.

[*Exit*]

CHORUS. The world is full of wonderful things
But none more so than man,
This prodigy who sails before the storm-winds,
330 Cutting a path across the sea's gray face
Beneath the towering menace of the waves.
And Earth, the oldest, the primeval god,
Immortal, inexhaustible Earth,
She too has felt the weight of his hand
As year after year the mules are harnessed
And plows go back and forwards in the fields.

Merry birds and forest beasts,
Fish that swim in the deep waters,
Are gathered into the woven nets
340 Of man the crafty hunter.
He conquers with his arts
The beasts that roam in the wild hill-country.
He tames the horses with their shaggy manes
Throwing a harness around their necks,
And the tireless mountain bull.

Speech he has made his own, and thought

That travels swift as the wind,
And how to live in harmony with others
In cities, and how to shelter himself
From the piercing frost, cold rain, when the open   350
Fields can offer but a poor night's lodging.
He is ever-resourceful; nothing that comes
Will find him unready, save Death alone.
Then he will call for help and call in vain,
Though often, where cure was despaired of, he has
    found one.

The wit of man surpasses belief,
It works for good and evil too;
When he honors his country's laws, and the right
He is pledged to uphold, then city
Hold up your head; but the man   360
Who yields to temptation and brings evil home
Is a man without a city; he has
No place in the circle of my hearth,
Nor any part in my counsels.

[*Enter* GUARD, *leading* ANTIGONE *prisoner*]

But what is this? The gods alone know.
Is it Antigone? She and no other.
Oh unhappy daughter of
Your wretched father Oedipus,
What is it? Have they arrested you?
Have you broken the royal commandment?   370
Has your foolishness brought you to this?
    GUARD. Here she is! This is the girl who did it!
We caught her burying him. But where is Creon?
    CHORUS. Here, coming from the palace, just in time.

[*Enter from the palace* CREON *with attendants*]

    CREON. Coming in time for what? What is it now?

GUARD. My lord, a man should never swear to any-
    thing.
Second thoughts belie the first. I could have sworn
I wouldn't have come back here again in a hurry
After the tongue-lashing you gave me last time.
380 But there's no pleasure like the one that comes
As a surprise, the last thing you expected.
So here I am, breaking my solemn oath,
Bringing this girl, who was caught performing
The final rites. We didn't draw lots this time.
This piece of luck belongs to me, and no-one else.
So now, my lord, she's yours, for you to examine
And question as you wish. I've done my duty;
It's someone else's problem from now on.
    CREON. This girl? Where did you take her? What was
      she doing?
390   GUARD. Burying the man. That's all there is to know.
    CREON. Are you serious? Do you know what you are
      saying?
    GUARD. I saw her burying the corpse, the thing
You had forbidden. What could be clearer than that?
    CREON. You saw her? Captured her redhanded?
      How?
    GUARD. It happened this way. When we returned to
      our posts
With your dreadful threats still ringing in our ears
We swept off every bit of dust that covered
The corpse, and left the rotting carcass bare,
Then sat down on the brow of a hill to windward
Where the stench couldn't reach us. We kept ourselves
400   lively
By threatening each other with what would happen
If anyone were careless in his duty.
And so time passed, until the sun's bright disk
Stood midway in the heavens, and the heat

Began to burn us. Suddenly a whirlwind
Raised a dust storm, a black blot on the sky,
Which filled the plain, played havoc with the leaves
Of every tree in sight, and choked the air.
We shut our eyes and bore it; heaven sends
These things to try us. When it had gone at last   410
There was the girl; she gave a shrill sharp cry
Like a bird in distress when it sees its bed
Stripped of its young ones and the nest deserted.
So she cried, when she saw the corpse left bare,
Raising her voice in grief, and calling down
Curses on the men who had done this thing.
Then at once she brought handfuls of dry dust,
Lifted a handsome vase, and poured from it
The three drink-offerings to crown the dead.
When we see it, out we run and close around her   420
In a moment. She was not at all put out.
We taxed her with what she had done, both then
And earlier; she admitted everything,
Which made me glad, but miserable too.
Nothing makes you happier than to get yourself
Out of trouble; but it's quite another thing
To get friends into it. But there's nothing
I wouldn't do, to keep myself from harm.
    CREON. You there; yes, you, who dare not look me in
      the face;
Do you admit this accusation or deny it?   430
    ANT. Oh, I admit it. I make no denial.
    CREON. [to the GUARD] Take yourself off, wherever
      you want to go,
A free man. You are cleared of a serious charge.
[to ANTIGONE] Now tell me, you, and keep your an-
      swers brief
Did you know there was an order forbidding this?
    ANT. Yes. How could I help it? Everybody knew.

CREON. And yet you dared to go against the law?

ANT. Why not? It was not Zeus who gave the order,
And Justice living with the dead below
440 Has never given men a law like this.
Nor did I think that your pronouncements were
So powerful that mere man could override
The unwritten and unfailing laws of heaven.
These live, not for today and yesterday
But for all time; they came, no man knows whence.
There is no man's resolve I fear enough
To answer to the gods for breaking these.
I knew that I must die—how could I help it?
Even without your edict; but if I die
450 Before my time is up, I count it gain.
For when a person lives as I do, in the midst
Of evils, what can death be but gain?
And so for me to happen on this fate
Is grief not worth a thought; but if I had left
My mother's son to lie a homeless corpse,
Then had I grieved. I do not grieve for this.
If what I do seems foolish in your sight
It may be that a fool condemns my folly.

CHORUS. This is her father's willful spirit in her,
460 Not knowing how to bend before the storm.

CREON. Come, you must learn that over-stubborn
    spirits
Are those most often humbled. Iron that has
Been hardened in the fire and cannot bend
You will find the first to snap and fly in pieces.
I have known high-mettled horses brought to order
By a touch on the bridle. Pride is not for those
Who live their lives at their neighbour's beck and call.
This girl was already schooled in insolence
When she disobeyed the official proclamation,
470 And now she adds insult to injury

By boasting of it, glorying in her crime.
I swear, she is the man and I the woman
If she keeps her victory and goes unpunished.
No! Even though she be my sister's child,
If she were bound to me by ties more close
Than anyone who shares our household prayers
She and that sister of hers will not escape
The ultimate fate; for I accuse her too
Of equal guilt in plotting this burial.
So go and call her. I saw her indoors just now   480
Delirious, not knowing what she was saying.

[*Exeunt* Attendants *to the palace*]

A guilty mind betrays itself beforehand
When men go plotting mischief in the dark.
But no less do I hate the criminal
Who is caught, and tries to glorify his crime.

    ANT. What more would you take from me than my
       life?
    CREON. Not a thing. When I have that, I have all I
       want.
    ANT. Then what are you waiting for? Your arguments
Fall on deaf ears; I pray they always will.
My loyalties are meaningless to you.   490
Yet, in the world's eyes, what could I have done
To earn me greater glory, than to give
My brother burial? Everybody here
Would cheer me, if they were not dumb with fear.
But royalty, among so many blessings,
Has power to say and do whatever it likes.
    CREON. These Thebans take a different view from
      yours.
    ANT. Not they. They only curb their tongues for your
      sake.

CREON. Then why be different? Are you not
  ashamed?

500 ANT. Ashamed? Of paying homage to a brother?
CREON. Was not the man he killed your brother too?
ANT. My brother, by one mother, by one father.
CREON. Then why pay honors hateful in his eyes?
ANT. The dead man will not say he finds them hate-
  ful.
CREON. When you honor him no higher than a trai-
  tor?
ANT. It was his brother died, and not his slave.
CREON. Destroying Thebes; while he died to protect
  it.
ANT. It makes no difference. Death asks these rites.
CREON. But a hero asks more honor than a traitor.
ANT. Who knows? The dead may find no harm in
510 this.
CREON. Even death cannot change hatred into love.
ANT. But I was born for love, and not for hate!
CREON. Then if you have to love, go down and love
The dead; while I live, no woman shall rule me!

[*Enter* Attendants *from the palace with* ISMENE]

CHORUS. Look, the gates open and Ismene comes
Weeping for love and sisterhood.
Her brows are clouded, shadowing
Her face flushed red, and teardrops
Fall on her lovely cheek.

520 CREON. And you, a viper lurking in my house,
Were sucking my life's blood, while I, unknowing,
Raised a twin scourge to drive me from my throne.
Come, answer me. Will you confess your share
In this burial, or deny all knowledge of it?
  ISM. I did it—if my sister will allow me.
Half the blame is mine. I take it on myself.

ANT. No! Justice will not let you! You refused,
And I denied you any part in it.

IsM. But now you are in trouble. I am not
Ashamed to ride the storm out at your side. 530

ANT. Who did it, Hades and the dead can witness.
I love not those who only talk of love.

IsM. No, sister, do not reject me. Let
Me die with you and sanctify the dead.

ANT. You shall not share my death. You had no hand
   in this.
Do not say you had. My death will be enough.

IsM. What joy have I in life when you are gone?

ANT. Ask Creon. All your care has been for him.

IsM. Why do you want to hurt me? It does no good.

ANT. You are right. If I mock you it is for my pain. 540

IsM. Then tell me how I can help you, even now.

ANT. Save yourself. I do not grudge you your escape.

IsM. Then is poor Ismene not to share your fate?

ANT. It was you who chose to live, and I to die.

IsM. At least I tried to move you from your choice.

ANT. One side approved your wisdom, the other
   mine.

IsM. And yet the offence is the same for both of us.

ANT. Be of good heart. You live; but I have been
Dead for a long time now, to serve the dead.

CREON. Here are two fools, one lately come to folly, 550
The other since the day that she was born.

IsM. Indeed, my lord, such sense as nature gives us
Is not for ever. It goes in time of trouble.

CREON. Like yours, when you chose bad friends and
   evil ways.

IsM. How can I bear to live without my sister?

CREON. Sister? You have no sister. She is dead.

IsM. But will you kill your son's appointed bride?

CREON. I will. My son has other fields to plow.

Ism. He will never love another as he loved her.

560   Creon. No son of mine will wed an evil woman.

Ism. Haemon, my dearest! How your father wrongs
    you!

Creon. Let us have no further talk of marriages.

Chorus. You will do it, then? You will rob your son
    of his bride?

Creon. Not I, but Death; yes, Death will break the
    match.

Chorus. The decision stands, then, that the girl must
    die?

Creon. For you, and me. Let us have no more delay.
Servants, take them inside. From this time on
They must be women, not let out alone.
Even the boldest of us turns and runs
570 The moment he can see death closing in.

    [*Exeunt* Attendants *with* Antigone *and* Ismene]

Chorus. Blessed are those whose days have not
    tasted evil,
For once the gods have set a house tottering
The curse will never fade, but continues
From generation unto generation,
Like a storm rolling over the dark waters
Driven by the howling Thracian gales,
Stirring black mud from the bottom of the sea;
And the wind-torn headlands answer back
In a sullen roar, as the storm breaks over them.

580 I look on the house of Labdacus
And see how, from time immemorial,
The sorrows of the living have been heaped upon
The sorrows of those that died before them.
One generation does not set another

561 **Haemon . . . wrongs you** it is uncertain whether this line
is spoken by Antigone or Ismene

Free, but some god strikes them down
And they have no means of deliverance.
Over the last root of the house of Oedipus
Shone a ray of hope; but now this too has been
Laid low by a handful of bloody dust
Demanded by the gods of the underworld,   590
By unthinking words, and the heart's delirium.

Zeus, what man's transgression can restrain your power,
When neither Sleep, that encompasses all things,
Nor the months' unwearied and god-ordered march
Can arrest it? You do not grow old with the years
But rule in shining splendor as Olympus' king.
As it was in the past, this law will hold
Tomorrow and until the end of time:
That mortal life has a limited capacity.
When it aims too high, then the curse will fall.   600

For Hope, whose territory is unbounded,
Brings comfort to many, but to many others
Insane desires and false encouragement.
A man may go blindly on his way
Then walk into the fire and burn himself,
And so disillusion comes.
In his wisdom, someone coined the famous saying
That when a god leads a man's mind on
To destruction, sooner or later he comes
To believe that evil is good, good evil,   610
And then his days of happiness are numbered.

[*Enter* HAEMON]

But here is Haemon, your youngest son.
Does he come to grieve for the doom that has fallen
Upon Antigone, his promised bride,

To complain of the marriage that is taken from him?
>CREON. We shall not need second sight to tell us
>>that.

My son, have you heard that sentence has been passed
On your betrothed? Are you here to storm at me?
Or have I your good will, whatever I do?
>HAEMON. Father, I am in your hands. You in your
>>wisdom
620 Lay down for me the paths I am to follow.
There is no marriage in the world
That I would put before my good advisor.
>CREON. Yes, keep this always in your heart, my son:
Accept your father's word as law in all things.
For that is why men pray to have
Dutiful children growing up at home,
To repay their father's enemies in kind
And honor those he loves no less than he does.
But a man is sowing troubles for himself
630 And enemies' delight—what else?—when he
Sires sons who bring no profit to their father.
So, my son, do not be led by passing fancy
To lose your head for a woman's sake. You know,
The warmth goes out of such embraces, when
An evil woman shares your home and bed.
False friends are deadlier than a festered wound.
So turn from her with loathing; let her find
A husband for herself among the dead.
For now that I have caught her, the only one
640 Of all the city to disobey me openly,
My people shall not see me break my word.
I shall kill her. Let her plead the sacred ties
Of kinship! If I bring up my own family
To flout me, there will be no holding others.
A man who sees his family obey him
Will have authority in public matters.

But if anyone offends, or violates the laws,
No word of praise shall he ever have from me.
Whoever the state appoints must be obeyed,
In little things or great things, right or wrong.   650
I should have confidence that such a man
Would be as good a ruler as a subject
And in a hail of spears would stand his ground
Where he was put, a comrade you could trust.
But disobedience is the worst of evils;
It is this that ruins cities, it is this
That makes homes desolate, turns brothers in arms
To headlong rout. But those who are preserved
Owe their lives, the greater part of them, to discipline.
And so we must stand up for law and order,   660
Not let ourselves be worsted by a woman.
If yield we must, then let us yield to a man.
Let no-one call us woman's underlings.

    CHORUS. Unless the years have robbed me of my wits
You seem to have sound sense in what you say.

    HAEMON. Father, the gods endow mankind with
      reason,
The highest quality that we possess.
It is not for me to criticize your words.
I could not do it, and would hate to try.
And yet, two heads are sometimes better than one;   670
At least, it is my place to watch, on your behalf,
All that men do and say and criticize.
Fear of your frown prevents the common man
From saying anything that would displease you,
But I can hear these murmurs in the dark,
The feeling in the city for this girl.
"No woman" they say "has ever deserved death less,
Or died so shamefully in a noble cause.
When her brother fell in the slaughter, she would not
Leave him unburied, to provide a meal   680

For carrion dogs or passing birds of prey.
Is she not, then, deserving golden honors?"
This is what men are whispering to each other.
Father, there is nothing dearer to my heart
Than your continuing prosperity.
What finer ornament could children have
Than a father's proud success—or he, than theirs?
So wear an open mind; do not suppose
That you are right, and everyone else is wrong.
690 A man who thinks he has monopoly
Of wisdom, no rival in speech or intellect,
Will turn out hollow when you look inside him.
However wise he is, it is no disgrace
To learn, and give way gracefully.
You see how trees that bend to winter floods
Preserve themselves, save every twig unbroken,
But those that stand rigid perish root and branch,
And also how the man who keeps his sails
Stretched taut, and never slackens them, overturns
700 And finishes his voyage upside down.
Let your anger rest; allow us to persuade you.
If a young man may be permitted his opinion
I should say it would be best for everyone
To be born omniscient; but otherwise—
And things have a habit of falling out differently—
It is also good to learn from good advice.

    CHORUS. My lord, if he speaks to the point you
       ought to listen,
And Haemon, you to him. There is sense on both sides.
    CREON. And is a man of my age to be taught
710 What I should think by one so young as this?
    HAEMON. Nothing that is not right; young though
       I may be,
You should judge by my behavior, not my age.
    CREON. What sort of behavior is it to honor rebels?

HAEMON. I would never suggest that the guilty should be honored.

CREON. And is she not infected with this disease?

HAEMON. The people of Thebes unanimously deny it.

CREON. Will the city tell me how I am to rule?

HAEMON. Listen to that! Who is being childish now?

CREON. Is the state to listen to any voice but mine?

HAEMON. There is no state, when one man is its master. 720

CREON. Is not the state supposed to be the ruler's?

HAEMON. You would do well as the monarch of a desert.

CREON. It seems the woman has a champion here.

HAEMON. Then you are the woman! It is you I care about!

CREON. Insolent cub! Will you argue with your father?

HAEMON. I will, when I see you falling into error.

CREON. Am I wrong to respect my own prerogatives?

HAEMON. It is no respect, when you offend the gods.

CREON. How contemptible, to give way to a woman!

HAEMON. At least I do not give way to temptation. 730

CREON. But every word you say is a plea for her.

HAEMON. And for you, and for me, and for the gods below.

CREON. You will never marry her this side of the grave.

HAEMON. Then she will die—and take somebody with her.

CREON. So! Do you dare to go so far? Are you threatening me?

HAEMON. Is it threatening, to protest a wrong decision?

CREON. You shall pay for this. A fine one to teach wisdom!

HAEMON. If you were not my father, I should call you a fool.

CREON. You woman's slave; do not try to wheedle me!

HAEMON. Would you stop everyone from speaking
740 but yourself?

CREON. Indeed! I tell you, by the gods above us,

You shall pay for using such language to your father.

[to the Attendants]

Bring this abomination out, and let her die
Here, in his presence, at her bridegroom's side.

HAEMON. No, she will never perish at my side,
So do not think it. From this moment on
Your eyes will never see my face again.
So rave away, to those who have more patience!

[Exit]

CHORUS. My lord, he has gone away in angry haste.
Young tempers are fierce when anything provokes
750 them.

CREON. Let him do or dream all men can do and more.

He shall never save those girls from punishment.

CHORUS. Do you mean to put the two of them to death?

CREON. You are right to ask. Not her whose hands are clean.

CHORUS. And how do you intend to kill the other?

CREON. I shall take her where nobody ever comes
And shut her in a rocky vault alive,
With the minimum of food that is permitted
To stop pollution falling on the city.

There she may pray to Death, the only god   760
She worships, and perhaps he may forgive her.
If not, she will learn—but when it is too late—
That honoring the dead is wasted effort.

[*Exit*]

CHORUS. Love, whom we fight but never conquer,
Love, the ravager of proud possessions
Who keep eternal vigilance
In the softness of a young girl's cheek,
You go wherever the wide seas go
And among the cottages of country-dwellers.
None of the immortal gods can escape you,   770
Nor man, whose life is as a single day,
And, to whoever takes you in, comes madness.

The minds of honest men you lead
Out of the paths of virtue to destruction.
Father is at odds with son
And it is you who set this quarrel in their hearts.
One glance from the eyes of a ready bride
Bright with desire, and a man is enslaved.
On the throne of the eternal laws
Love has a place, for there the goddess Aphrodite   780
Decides men's fates, and there is no withstanding her.

[*Enter* Attendants *with* ANTIGONE *bound*]

It is my turn now; at a sight like this
The voice of the laws cannot hold me back
Or stop the tears from pouring down my cheeks.
Here comes Antigone, on her way
To the bridal-chamber where all must go to rest.
    ANT. See me, citizens of my fatherland, as I go out 790

780 **Aphrodite** goddess of love, or, more accurately, of sexual
desire

On my last journey; as I look my last on the sunlight,
Never to see it again; Death, who puts all to sleep,
Takes me as I am,
With life still in me, to the shores of the midnight lake,
A bride with no choir to accompany her way,
With no serenade at the bedroom door;
I am to marry with the King of Darkness!

    CHORUS. And so you go with honor and praise
Below to the caverns of the dead;
No sickness has wasted you away,
You do not pay the wages of the sword,
But will go to death a law unto yourself
800 As no human being has done before you.

        ANT. I have heard of one, a stranger among us from
           Phrygia,
Tantalus' daughter, and her sad end on Mount Sipylus,
Growing slowly into stone as a tree is wrapped with
    ivy.
And the story goes
That her body pines in unceasing snow and rain
And tears from her streaming eyes pour upon her
    breast.
Her fate is mine; like her I go to rest.

    CHORUS. But she was a goddess, born of gods,
And we are mortals, mortal born.
810 When a woman has to die, it is
A great distinction, for her to share
The lot of those who are one removed from gods,
Both here, and in the manner of her death.

    ANT. Oh, you make fun of me! Gods of my fathers!

792 **A bride . . . bedroom door** according to Greek custom
bride and groom were accompanied home by singing friends,
who also sang outside the wedding chamber in the evening
801 **Tantalus' daughter** Niobe, daughter of the king of Phrygia
in Asia Minor, turned into stone as punishment for boasting
herself superior to the gods

Must you laugh in my face? Can you not wait till I
    am gone?
Oh, my city; Thebans, proud in your possessions;
Chariot-thundering plain, you at least will bear witness
How no friends mourn for my passing, by what laws
I go to my rock-barred prison, my novel tomb.
Luckless Antigone, an alien in both worlds,   820
Among the living and among the dead!
    CHORUS. You have driven yourself to the furthest
    limit of daring
And run, my child, against the high throne
Where justice sits; and great has been your fall.
Perhaps you are paying the price of your father's sin.
    ANT. You have touched the memory bitterest in my
    mind,
The dirge for my father that is never finished,
For the fate of us all, the famous house of Labdacus.
Oh, the curse born
In a mother's bed; doomed mother, sleeping with her
    son,   830
My father. Poor Antigone, what parents brought you
Into this world! Now I go to join them, accursed,
    unwed.
Oh, my brother, how ill-fated was your marriage.
Your dead hand has reached out to destroy the living.
    CHORUS. Pious actions are a sort of piety.
But a man who has authority in his keeping
Can permit no offence against authority.
Your own willful temper has destroyed you.
    ANT. Friendless, unwept, without a wedding song,
They call for me, and I must tread my road.   840
Eye of heaven, light of the holy sun,

833 **Oh, my brother** not Oedipus, but Polyneices, whose marriage with the daughter of the king of Argos had cemented the alliance against Thebes

I may look on you no longer.
There is no friend to lament my fate,
No-one to shed a tear for me.

[*Enter* CREON]

CREON. Let me tell you, if songs and dirges before
    dying
Did any good, we should never hear the end of them.
Take her, and be quick about it. Lock her up
In her cavern tomb, as I have ordered you,
And leave her alone—to die, if she prefers,
850 Or live in her tomb, for that will be her home.
Whatever becomes of her our hands are clean.
But in this world she has a place no longer.
    ANT. Tomb, bridal-chamber, my eternal home
Hewn from the rock, where I must go to meet
My own, those many who have died, and been
Made welcome by Persephone in the shadow-world.
I am the last, my death the worst of all
Before my allotted span of years has run.
But as I go I have this hope in heart,
860 That my coming may be welcome to my father,
My mother; welcome, dearest brother, to you.
For when you died, with my own hands I washed
And robed your bodies, and poured offerings
Over your graves. Now this is my reward,
Polyneices, for rendering such services to you.
Yet wisdom would approve my honoring you.
If I were a mother; if my husband's corpse
Were left to rot, I never should have dared
Defy the state to do what I have done.
870 What principle can justify such words?

856 **Persephone** queen of the dead   867 **If I were a mother
. . . born to me again** this passage is possibly spurious, and
omitted by some editors

Why, if my husband died I could take another;
Someone else could give me a child if I lost the first;
But Death has hidden my mother and father from me.
No brother can be born to me again.
Such was the principle by which I chose
To honor you; and for this Creon judges me guilty
Of outrage and transgression, brother mine!
And now he seizes me to lead me off,
Robbed of my bride-bed and my marriage song.
I shall never marry, never be a mother.   880
And so, in misery, without a friend,
I go still living to the pit of death.
Which one of heaven's commandments have I broken?
Why should I look to the gods any longer
After this? To whom am I to turn for help
When doing right has branded me a sinner?
If the gods approve what is happening to me,
After the punishment I shall know my fault,
But if my judges are wrong, I wish them no worse
Than what they have unjustly done to me.   890

    CHORUS. Still the same tempestuous spirit
Carrying her along.

    CREON. Then those who are charged with taking her
Shall have cause to repent their slowness.

    ANT. Oh, that word has brought me
Very near my death.

    CREON. I can offer you no hope.
Your punishment stands unchanged.

    ANT. City of my father in the land of Thebes,   900
The time has come, they take me away.
Look, princes of Thebes; this is the last
Daughter of the house of your kings.
See what I suffer, and at whose hands,
For doing no less than heaven bids us do.

[*Exeunt* Attendants, *leading off* ANTIGONE]

CHORUS. So Danae in her beauty endured the change
From the bright sky to the brazen cell,
And there she was hidden, lost to the living world.
Yet she was of proud birth too, my daughter,
And the seed of Zeus was trusted to her keeping
910 That fell in golden rain.
But the power of fate is terrible.
Wealth cannot keep you from its reach, nor war,
Nor city walls, nor the dark sea-beaten ships.

And the king of the Edonians, the fiery-tempered
Son of Dryas, was held in bondage
For his savage taunts, at Dionysus' will,
Clapped in a rocky cell; and so the full
Flowering of his madness passed from him gradually
And he came to recognize
920 The god he had insulted in his frenzy.
    He had sought to stop the women when the god was in
        them
    And the Bacchic torches, and enraged the piping
        Muses.

And by the Dark Rocks at the meeting of two waters
Lie the shores of Bosporos and Thracian Salmydessos.

905 **Danae** the chorus adduce from mythology parallels to Antigone's plight. **Danae** was imprisoned by her father in a brazen
tower to avert a prophecy that she would bear a son who would
grow up to kill him. But Zeus, king of the gods, appeared to
her in a shower of golden rain and fathered her son Perseus,
who grew up to fulfil the prophecy **Lycurgus** son of Dryas
persecuted the worshippers of Dionysus, and as punishment for
his insolence was driven mad by the god and died **Cleopatra**
married **Phineus**, King of Salmydessos in Thrace, and bore
him two sons. Phineus later imprisoned her and took a new
wife, who blinded the boys   923 **Dark Rocks** at the entrance
to what is now the Black Sea   924 **Bosporos** narrow strip of
water separating Greece from Asia Minor

Here was a sight for the eyes
Of the city's neighbour, Ares—
The two sons of Phineus, blinded
By stepmother's fury, their sightless eyes
Appealing for vengeance, calling down a curse
On her bloody hands and the shuttle turned dagger.   930

Pining in grief they bewailed their cruel fate.
How sad their mother's marriage; but her line
Went back to the ancient family
Of Erechtheus—she was a child
Of the North Wind, nursed in distant caves,
Who played with her father's storms, a child of the
     gods
Running swift as a steed upon the high hills.
Yet on her too the gray Fates laid their hand, my
     daughter.

[*Enter* TEIRESIAS, *led by a boy*]

TEIRESIAS. Princes of Thebes, we have come here
     side by side,
One pair of eyes for both of us. That is how   940
Blind men must walk, supported by a guide.
  CREON. What news have you for us, old Teiresias?
  TEIR. I will tell you. Listen when the prophet speaks.
  CREON. I have never yet disregarded your advice.
  TEIR. And so have kept Thebes safely on her course.
  CREON. I know my debt to you, and acknowledge it.
  TEIR. Then listen. Once more you stand on the
     verge of doom.
  CREON. What do you mean? I shudder at your
     words.

926 **Ares** god of war: see n. on *Oedipus the King* v. 190   934
Erechtheus legendary king of Athens

TEIR. You will know, when you hear the warnings
  of my art.
950 As I took my place upon my ancient seat
  Of augury, where all the birds come flocking,
  I heard a noise I had never heard before,
  Their cries distorted in a scream of fury,
  And I knew that they were clawing, killing each other;
  The whirring of wings told a tale too clear.
  I was frightened, and went at once to light the altar
  And offer sacrifice; but from my offerings
  No flame sprang up. Fat melted on the thighs
  And oozed in slow drops down to quench the embers
960 And smoked and spluttered; and the gall was scattered
  Into the air. The streaming thighs were raw,
  Bare of the fat which once enfolded them.
  And so my rites had failed. I asked a sign
  And none was given, as I learnt from this boy here.
  He is my guide, as I am guide to others.
  Your counsels brought this sickness on our state.
  The altars of our city and our homes
  All are defiled by dogs and birds of prey
  Who feed on Oedipus' unhappy son.
970 And so the gods no longer accept our prayers,
  Our sacrifices, our burnt offerings.
  The birds no longer warn us with their cries;
  They have drunk the fat blood of a slaughtered man.
  Think on these things, my son. To err is human,
  But when we err, then happy is the man
  Who is not stubborn, and has sense enough
  To remedy the fault he has committed.
  Give the dead his due, and do not stab a man
  When he is down. What good to kill him twice?
980 I have your interests at heart, and speak
  To help you. No advisor is more welcome
  Than when you profit from his good advice.

CREON. You circle me like archers, all of you,
And I am made your target! Even the prophets
Conspire against me. They have long been using me
As merchandise, a thing to buy and sell!
If profit is what you seek, go look abroad!
There is silver in Sardis, gold in India.
But you will not bury this man in his grave,
No, not if the eagles of great Zeus himself   990
Should lay his flesh before their master's throne.
Not even that defilement frightens me
Enough to bury him, for well I know
No human being can defile the gods.
The wisest of us, old Teiresias,
Sink to the depths, when they hide their evil thoughts
In fair-phrased speeches for the sake of money.
    TEIR. If men only knew, would only realize—
    CREON. Knew what? Another pronouncement! Let
        us hear!
    TEIR. Good counsel is worth more than wordly
        riches.   1000
    CREON. Just as stupidity is the greatest harm.
    TEIR. Yet that is the sickness that has tainted you.
    CREON. I do not want to call a prophet names.
    TEIR. But you do, when you say my prophecies are
        false.
    CREON. Men of your tribe were always money-
        seekers.
    TEIR. And men of yours have always been dictators.
    CREON. Have you forgotten you are speaking to your
        king?
    TEIR. No. It was because of me that you saved
        Thebes.
    CREON. You are a wise prophet but in love with evil.

---

988 **Sardis** city of Asia Minor containing the royal treasury

TEIR. You will move me to tell the unutterable se-
1010 cret.

CREON. Tell it—as long as there is no profit in it!

TEIR. I do not think so—as far as you are concerned.

CREON. You will make no money out of my decision.

TEIR. Then listen well. Before the sun's swift wheels
Have numbered many more days of your life,
You will surrender corpse for corpses, one
Begotten from the seed of your own loins,
Because you have sent this world to join the next
And cruelly lodged the living in the grave,
1020 But keep Death's property on earth, unburied,
Robbed of its honor, an unhallowed corpse.
This is not for you to say, nor for the gods
In heaven, but in doing this you wrong them.
And so the Avengers, Furies sent by Death
And by the gods, lie in waiting to destroy you
And snare you in the evils you have worked.
So watch, and you will see if I am bribed
To say these things. Before much time is out
The cries of men and womenfolk will fill your house.
1030 And hatred rises against you in every city
Whose mangled sons were left for burial
To dogs, or beasts, or birds of prey, who bore
Their stinking breath to every soldier's home.
Archer you call me; then these are the arrows
I send into your heart, since you provoke me,
Sure arrows; you will not escape their sting.
Boy, take me to my home again, and leave him
To vent his fury on some younger man,
And learn to moderate his tongue, and bear
1040 A better spirit in his breast than now.

[*Exit*]

1024 **Furies** supernatural pursuers of the wrongdoer

CHORUS. He has gone, my lord; his prophecies were
   fearful.
As long as I remember, since my hair
Has turned from black to white, this man has never
Made one false prophecy about our city.
   CREON. I know it as well as you. My mind is trou-
      bled.
To yield is fatal; but to resist and bring
A curse on my proud spirit—that too is hard.
   CHORUS. Son of Menoeceus, you must listen to good
      advice.
   CREON. What's to be done? Tell me and I will do it.
   CHORUS. Go free the girl from her prison in the rocks 1050
And give the corpse an honorable tomb.
   CREON. Is this your advice? You think that I should
      yield?
   CHORUS. Yes, lord, as quickly as you can. The gods
Move fast to cut short man's stupidity.
   CREON. It is hard; but I resign my dear resolve.
We cannot fight against necessity.
   CHORUS. Go do it now; do not leave it to another.
   CREON. I will go as I am. Servants, be off with you,
Each and every one; take axes in your hands
And go to the hill you can see over there.   1060
Now that my judgment has been reversed
I shall be there to free her, as I imprisoned her.
Perhaps after all the gods' ways are the best
And we should keep them till our lives are done.

[Exit]

   CHORUS. You who are known by many names,
Who blessed the union of Cadmus' daughter,
Begotten by Zeus the Thunderer, guarding

1066 **Cadmus' daughter** Semele: see n. on *Oedipus the King,*
v. 200

The land of Italy famed in story,
King of Eleusis, in the land-locked plain
1170 Of Deo where the wanderer finds welcome,
Bacchus whose home is Thebes, mother-city of Bacchanals,
By Ismenus' tranquil waters where the fierce dragon's
teeth were sown.

The fitful gleam of the torchlight finds you
Amid the smoke on the slopes of the forked mountains
Where tread your worshippers, the nymphs
Of Corycia, by Castalia's stream.
From Nysa's ivy-mantled slopes,
From the green shore carpeted with vines
You come, and they are no human lips that cry
Your name, as you make your progress through the
1180   ways of Thebes.

For it is she you honor above all other cities,
And your mother too, who died by a bolt from heaven.
And now the whole city labors under
This grievous malady, come with healing feet
Down from the slopes of Parnassus or the sounding
sea.

Conductor of the stars, whose breath is made of fire,
Lord of the voices that cry aloud in the night,
Son born of Zeus, appear to us, oh lord,
With the Thyiads your servants who in nightly aban-
don

1069 **Eleusis** home of the mystery-cult devoted to Demeter,
goddess of the crops, and her daughter Persephone. The worship of Dionysus had infiltrated into this rite   1070 **Deo** Demeter   1072 **By Ismenus'** . . . **were sown** see n. on *Oedipus
the King*, v. 1   1076 **Corycia** cave on Mt. Parnassus   **Castalia**
fountain on Mt. Parnassus sacred to the Muses   1077 **Nysa**
legendary scene of the nursing of Dionysus

Dance before you, Iacchus, the bringer of all bless-
    ings. 1090

[*Enter* MESSENGER]

MESSENGER. You who live by Amphion's and Cad-
    mus' walls,
No man's estate is ever so assured
That I would set it down as good or bad.
Fortune can raise us, fortune cast us down,
Depending on our luck, from day to day,
But for how long? No man can see the future.
For Creon was once blessed, as I count blessings;
He saved the land of Cadmus from its enemies,
Became its sole and undisputed king
And ruled, proud father of a princely line. 1100
Now everything is gone. A man who forfeits
All of life's pleasures I can count no longer
Among the living, but as dead in life.
So stack your house with treasures as you will
And live in royal pomp; when joy is absent
I would not give the shadow of a breath
For all the rest, compared with joy alone.
    CHORUS. What is this new royal grief you come to
        tell us?
    MESS. Death; and the living must answer to the
        dead.
    CHORUS. Who killed? And who has been killed?
        Tell us. 1110
    MESS. Haemon, and by a hand he knew too well.
    CHORUS. By his father's hand? Or was it by his own?
    MESS. His own, in anger for his father's murder.
    CHORUS. Oh prophet, how much truth was in your
        words.

1091 **Amphion** legendary musician whose lyre-playing charmed
the stones to build a wall around Thebes

MESS. That is how things are. For the rest you must
decide.

[*Enter* EURYDICE]

CHORUS. And here is Eurydice, the unhappy wife
Of Creon; she is coming from the palace.
　EURYDICE. People of Thebes, I heard what you were
　　saying
As I was going from my house to offer
1220 Devotions at the goddess Pallas' shrine.
I stood there with my hand about to draw
The bolt, and my ears were greeted by this tale
Of family disaster. Terrified,
I fell back swooning in my servants' arms.
But tell again what you were telling then.
The first grief is over. I shall listen now.
　MESS. Dear lady, I shall tell you what I saw
Omitting nothing, exactly as it happened.
Why should I give false comfort? You would soon
1230 Know I was lying. Truth is always best.
I attended on your husband to direct his way
Across the plain, where Polyneices' corpse,
Mangled by dogs, still lay unburied.
We prayed the goddess of the roads, and Pluto,
To have mercy on us and restrain their wrath,
Performed the ritual washing of the corpse,
Cut branches and cremated what was left of him
And raised a hillock of his native soil
Above him; then made for the cavern, where the girl
1240 Waited for Death to share her rocky bed.
Far off, one of us heard a piercing cry
Coming from that unholy bridal chamber
And came to report it to our master Creon.

1134 **Pluto** god of the underworld

As he approached, a cry of anguish came
To greet him, half-heard words; he groaned aloud
And in his grief said "Creon, you are doomed;
Can my fear be true? Is the path I tread today
To be the bitterest path I ever trod?
The voice that greets me is my son's; men, run ahead,
Make for the tomb; there is an opening   1150
Where someone has wrenched the stones away.
 Squeeze inside
To the cell-mouth, see if it is Haemon's voice
I hear, or if the gods are mocking me."
And so, at our despairing master's bidding,
We made the search, and in the farthest corner
Of the tomb we saw her, hanged by the neck
In a noose of twisted linen, soft as silk,
While Haemon stood with his arms clasped round her
 waist
Weeping for his bride now with the dead,
For his father's actions and his foredoomed marriage. 1160
When he saw him his father gave a fearful cry
And went to him and called to him through his tears
"Oh Haemon, what is this that you have done?
What has possessed you? Have you gone insane?
Come out, my son, I beg you, I implore you."
But the boy glared back at him wild-eyed,
Spat in his face, and without a word of answer
Drew his cross-hilted sword and thrust at him
But missed, as he jumped aside. Then in wild remorse
The poor wretch threw his weight upon the point   1170
And drove it half into his side. As long as sense
Was left him, he clasped the girl in a limp embrace
And as his breath came hard, a jet of blood
Spurted from his lips, and ran down her pallid cheek.
The bodies lie in each other arms. He has
Claimed his bride—in the next world, not in this—

And he has given proof to all mankind
That of all human ills, bad counsel is the worst.

[*Exit* Eurydice *to the palace*]

CHORUS. What would you make of this? Eurydice
180   Has vanished without a word, good or bad.
        MESS. It alarms me too. Yet I nourish the hope
That now she knows her loss she does not think it
            proper
To mourn in public, but has gone inside
To set her maids to mourn for her bereavement.
She has learnt discretion and will not be foolish.
        CHORUS. I am not so sure. To me this unnatural
            silence
Is as ominous as the wildest excess of grief.
        MESS. Well, I shall go in and see, in case
She is keeping some dark purpose hidden from us
190   In her grief-torn heart. You are right to be concerned.
It is just as dangerous to be too quiet.

[*Exit*]

CHORUS. But here is Creon coming himself
Bringing testimony all too plain,
The work of his and no other's madness,
If I may speak out, and his own wrongdoing.

[*Enter* CREON *with servants bearing the body of*
HAEMON]

CREON. Oh deadly end of stubborn sins
Born in the blindness of understanding!
See here, a son dead, a father who killed him.
Oh the fatal workings of my mind;
200   My son, to die so young,
So soon to be taken from me

By my folly, not by yours.

CHORUS. Perhaps you see now too late what was
best.

CREON. Yes, I have learned my bitter lesson.
Some god must have chosen that moment
To crush me under his heavy hand
And hurl me into cruelty's ways,
Biding roughshod over all I held dear.
Oh, mankind, you were born to suffer!

[*Enter* SECOND MESSENGER *from the palace*]

MESSENGER. Master, you do not come empty-handed;
but there is   1210
More in store for you. You bear one load of grief
But soon you will see another, in your home.

CREON. My grief is here; is any worse to come?

MESS. Your wife is dead—true mother to her son
To the last, poor lady—by a wound still fresh.

CREON. Oh Death, ever-open door,
Do you have no mercy on me?
You who bring this tale of death and sorrow
What is this you are saying to me?
What news is this, my boy?   1220
My wife is dead? One more
To add to the pile of corpses?

MESS. See for yourself. It is no longer hidden.

[*The body of* EURYDICE *is brought out*]

CREON. Oh, here is another, a second blow.
What has fate in store for me after this?
I have but this moment lifted
My child in my arms, and again
I see a corpse brought out to greet me.
Oh wretched mother; oh my child.

MESS. There she lies at the altar, knife-point in her
    heart.
1230 She mourned the noble fate of Megareus,
The first to die, then his; then closed her eyes
For ever, and with her dying breath called down
A curse on you for murdering her sons.

    CREON. I am shaken with fear. Will nobody take
His two-edged sword and run me through?
For, oh, I am sick at heart.
Sorrow has made me his own.

    MESS. Yes, she whose body you see lying here
1240 Laid the deaths of both sons at your door.

    CREON. And what was the violent manner of her
      leaving?

    MESS. Her own hand drove the knife into her heart
When she had heard them singing her son's dirge.

    CREON. Nobody else can bear the guilt,
No-one can take the blame from me.
I killed you, I, your unhappy father,
This is the truth.
Servants, take me away from this place.
Let me stay not a moment longer.
1250 Creon has ceased to exist.

    CHORUS. Good advice, if there can be any good in
      evil.
In present trouble the shortest way is best.

    CREON. Let it come. What better fate could I ask
Than the fate which ushers in my life's last day?
Let it come, the best of all;
Let me never see tomorrow's dawn.

1231 **Megareus** a minor incident in the siege of Thebes, which
Sophocles could expect his audience to know. Megareus, son
of Creon, sacrificed himself in an attempt to appease the gods'
wrath against the city

CHORUS. All in its proper time. We have things to
    see to
Here and now. The future is in other hands.
    CREON. But everything I want was in that prayer.
    CHORUS. Save your prayers. Whatever is going to
    happen   1260
Is already fated. Nobody can change it.
    CREON. Come, take this hot-headed fool away,
A fool who killed you, my son, in my blindness,
And you too, who are lying here; poor fool.
I do not know
Which way I am to take, where to lean;
My hands can do nothing right;
I am crushed beneath my fate.

[*Exit*]

    CHORUS. To be happy it is first of all necessary
To be wise, and always remember   1270
To give the gods their due.
The measure of a proud man's boasting
Shall be the measure of his punishment
And teach him late in life
The nature of true wisdom.

BIBLIOGRAPHY

THE GREEK THEATER

Arnott, P. D., *An Introduction to the Greek Theatre* (St. Martin's, 1958).

Bieber, M., *The History of the Greek and Roman Theater* (Princeton, 1939).

SOPHOCLES AND THE DEVELOPMENT OF TRAGEDY

Kirkwood, G. M., *A Study of Sophoclean Drama* (Cornell, 1958).

Kitto, H. D. F., *Greek Tragedy* (Doubleday, 1954).

Waldock, A. J. A., *Sophocles the Dramatist* (Cambridge, 1951).

Webster, T. B. L., *An Introduction to Sophocles* (Oxford, 1936).

Whitman, C. H., *Sophocles* (Harvard, 1951).

THE PLAYS

The standard annotated text is that of Sir Richard Jebb (Cambridge, 1883-1906) which offers the Greek text, literal translation, and copious notes. Sir John Sheppard's *The Oedipus Tyrannus of Sophocles* (Cambridge, 1920) is arranged on the same plan and prefaced by valuable chapters on the background and structure of the play.

Among a number of contemporary translations, *Sophocles: Three Tragedies* (Chicago, Complete Greek Tragedies series, 1954) has a short but stimulating introduction.

107